GRACE before MEALS™

Recipes for Family Life

Father Leo E. Patalinghug
with Stella Snyder

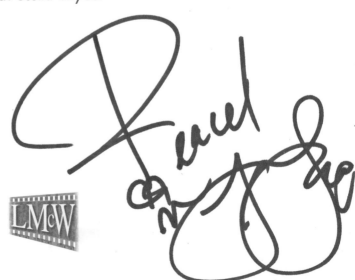

LMcW

Published by:
Leo McWatkins Films
10950 Gilroy Road
Suite J
Hunt Valley, MD 21031
Phone: 410-667-4710 Fax: 410-667-4328
www.leomcwatkins.com

ISBN 978-0-9796035-0-1

First Edition

TABLE OF CONTENTS
Grace Before Meals
RECIPES FOR FAMILY LIFE

INTRODUCTION
Grace Before Meals
RECIPES FOR FAMILY LIFE

So he commanded the skies above; the doors of heaven he opened.

God rained manna upon them for food; bread from heaven he gave them.

All ate a meal fit for heroes; food he sent in abundance.

PSALM 78: 23-25

If food is one of God's bountiful blessings to His people, it only makes sense that the preparation of that food can also be a blessing, especially to our families. There are countless opportunities to teach and learn about God in every aspect of our relationship with food. From our earliest years, we can understand the miracle of growth as we sow seeds and watch them flourish under our watchful care, or prop a potato over a container of water and watch it sprout roots and leaves. As grandparents, we can pass on traditions flavored with secret recipes for the special cakes and pies that have been family favorites for longer than anyone remembers. Or perhaps we can tell the stories of times when God showed His goodness by providing "manna" for our family in times of trouble.

In between these two extremes of discovery and remembrance, the time spent in a kitchen preparing a meal as a family offers unmatchable opportunities to learn and talk about much more than measuring flour or chopping vegetables. Conversations come easily in a kitchen, and both parents and children often find it safer to have a heart-to-heart talk if they don't have to be eye-to-eye while they're doing it.

The inevitable shared successes and failures that come with the process of creating sauces and soufflés also serve a deeper purpose.

They shrink the gaps in relationships stretched by packed schedules.

This edition of *Grace Before Meals* was created especially for families. Without being "preachy" or boring, parents can use these themed meals—from the obvious like Thanksgiving to the less obvious like World Day of the Sick—to provide food for the soul as well as the stomach. Along with short essays, scriptures, and menus, you'll find dozens of suggestions for transforming mealtime lessons into actions that respect children and teens, acknowledge their unique needs, and reinforce their connection to the family.

The best teachers, especially parents, never stop being students themselves. So it is our hope that you will be surprised by what you discover as you go through each chapter. Our prayer is that your own gifts and experience will be enriched as both you and your children learn how to prepare, serve, and enjoy meals that richly satisfy long after the meal is over and they have grown into adults.

Using This Book:

Experiencing true grace before a meal is not limited to the prayer families say before they eat. It happens when you come together to cook, talk, and share blessings at your table! Here are a few hints to help make *Grace Before Meals: Recipes for Family Life* even more effective:

Satisfying our Hungry Hearts

Each chapter begins with a brief passage from Sacred Scripture followed by a lesson or thought about the suggested event or holy day/holiday. From there, families have an opportunity to make the celebration happen by coming together to create not only a delicious meal, but great memories, too.

Let's Talk

This list of questions can help families start conversations about the things that matter most to them, namely, what each of you believes. Some feel that families should not talk about religion, sports, or politics at the dinner table. I wholeheartedly disagree! These proposed questions allow your family to talk without fear, but with love!

Let's Listen

God's Word is alive and enlivening! These Scripture references give families an extra opportunity to consider God's perspective on family life and holidays, or as some originally called them, "holy days." Some families may even want to begin their family meal with one of the suggested passages or use it as a meditation throughout the week. This section reminds us that God does speak to us in our hearts, so let's leave room for Him at our table.

Let's Cook

The proposed menus come from my experiences while traveling, dining with my family, friends and parishioners, and experimenting to satisfy my own cravings. Don't feel obligated to use these exact menus in this exact order. Feel free to mix the recipes and ingredients based on your family's taste buds, cravings, and dietary restrictions. It is my hope that these recipes can inspire you to travel deeply in the journeys you all take in life and to experiment with your family's cravings as well.

Fun Facts

Fun facts make life fun! That's why we've highlighted some of our family-friendly ideas, cooking tips, and other fun facts. We hope you enjoy the colorful and easy-to-read format, because we want to help make your family experience fun, as a matter of fact!

Journal About Your Journey

One of our goals in creating this book was to help you create new memories for your family. That's why we've made a special section of the book just for that. Feel free to include pictures or write some notes to help you keep the memories around, unlike leftovers!

Happy Feasting!

Acknowledgments

My Heavenly Family: Father, Son, & Holy Spirit, Mother Mary, my Patrons, Saint Leo the Great, Saint Joseph, and the whole Communion of Saints (that just about covers them).

My Earthly Family: My most loving mother and father, Carlos and Fe; my supportive and loving siblings, Maria, Carlos, and Angelica; my grandparents; uncles; aunts; cousins; the best in-laws a guy could have; and the coolest and cutest nieces and nephews!

My Church Family: The former Archbishop of Baltimore, Cardinal William Keeler; his successor, Archbishop Edwin O'Brien; the parish family of St. John Catholic Church in Westminster, Maryland; my home parish of St. Rose of Lima in Baltimore; my supportive brother priests who suggested I share my passion for kitchen conversation with others: Rev. Msgr. Joseph Luca, Rev. Msgr. Arthur Valenzano, Fr. Erik Arnold, Fr. Brian Nolan, Fr. Michael DeAscanis, The Daughters of St. Paul for their enthusiasm and inspiration; and all of my brother priests, seminarians, and religious women and men who have shared my meals and my desire to help bring families closer to the real Banquet to come.

The Grace Before Meals Family: Tim Watkins for his daily commitment to God's work (and not to forget, for picking up the tab)! His wife, Susan, and their beautiful children; Stella Snyder, whose gift with words and writing is a real gift from God; Shelly Mulligan for keeping the project on track; Phill Bednarik and Mike Little for their creative eye and designs; Dan (Riz) Fleuette for his skill in operations; Don Aboff for his print expertise; Chris Beutler for his enthusiasm; the Hullett Family, who opened their home to film the pilot episode of our companion TV series; and the many individuals and families who opened their kitchens and pantries to help us put the *Grace Before Meals* philosophy to the test: Jason Bloom, George Convery, Jim Decker, Laura Fick, Katrina Heiser, Kate Karbowniczek, Kathy Knapick, Liz Massanopoli, Matt McDermott, the Mohideen Family, the Mulligan Family, Tien Pasco, Nicholas and Kate Piché, Gay Pinder, Evgeniya Prokhno, Kate Reckner, Jaime and Jesse Robertson, Kathy Sirkis, Julianna Wittig, Suzanne Cannole, Teresa Hughes, Dottie Dunn, Gail Buss, Nancy Wolfinger, Margaret Fletcher, Theresa Greene, Susan Foley, Teresa D'Epagnier, Donna Walker, Myra Corbit, Sue Berger, Donna Kelly, Sue Hopkins, Sharon Beaver, Susan Lakomy, Edie Foster, Vicki Mascalco, Dawn Walsh, Billy Schroeder, The O'Donnells, Donna Brown, and Greg Hutsell.

CHAPTER 1

Fresh Starts

So whoever is in Christ is a new creation: the old things have passed away;

behold, new things have come. And all this is from God, who has reconciled us

to himself through Christ and given us the ministry of reconciliation.

2 CORINTHIANS 5: 17-18

Happy New Year! Have you ever wondered why we make such a big deal out of New Year's Day? Even before there were marathon bowl games, Mummers parades and downtown fireworks shimmering off skyscrapers, we welcomed in the new year with bells and toasts and a quick look back before we embraced the new year with all its possibilities.

Whether we realize it, our celebrations mark something far more important than a change in the calendar. They commemorate something that is unique to our faith and to American culture—the new day and the opportunity to live very differently than we have in the past.

The verse at the top of this page says a remarkable thing about God. When we tell Him the truth about ourselves, He reconciles us to Himself. He changes the course of our lives so that we are no longer turning away from Him but running toward Him. When we are adopted into His family, we're truly new creations. Think about it—when He looks at us after we have sought forgiveness, He sees us wearing Christ's robes, graced by His gift of salvation. Our old failures are forgiven. God gives us a fresh start. And as if that weren't enough, He promises us one fresh start after another, every time we ask, no matter how many times we ask. Beyond that, He asks us to become reconcilers ourselves. He wants us to make that ministry our number one priority!

We demonstrate our understanding of God's reconciliation in our lives when we take a look at ourselves and decide there are some things we'd like to do differently. We might identify old habits we want to get rid of and new habits we want to develop. We might make a list of New Year's resolutions or a more comprehensive set of

> *The new year represents the opportunity to live very differently than we have in the past.*

goals for ourselves and our families. We might decide to make changes in small steps, or we might be ready to turn a dream into a reality.

The wonderful thing is that we have the freedom to reinvent ourselves by truly becoming ourselves. In our society, we applaud those who have overcome adversity of all kinds and worked to make their lives better. We do not believe in any kind of caste system. In fact, we are more likely to appreciate the "self-made" entrepreneur than someone who lives off wealth accumulated by an ancestor.

The same is true for growing up. In their tween and teen years, young people can be really hard on themselves. Sometimes they misread the learning process as an unchangeable assessment of their potential. The urging of parents, teachers, or coaches who see so much potential in their children can be heard as criticism. Teens may not yet grasp the greatness of God, His ability to take away every sin we bring to Him, and His power to keep us from those sins that seem to ensnare us. You can help your kids through this time by emphasizing the positives and the new opportunities they'll encounter in the years ahead. Everybody needs somebody to pay attention to their successes. Why not share your own resolutions for this year with your children? You can cheer each other on as you all work on becoming new people in the new year!

This feast celebrates how Mary is truly the Mother of God. It is a reminder of what Grace did for a simple virgin.

Let's Talk

If you were creating a reel of highlights from last year, what would be on it?

What experience was the most fun? What accomplishment made you the most proud?

If you could do one new thing this year, what would it be? What is standing between you and that goal? How could you remove or move around those obstacles?

If you were writing goals or resolutions for your family, what would top the list?

What would be one step toward achieving it?

Do you know somebody whose life is very different now than it was five years ago? How did that change come about?

If your parents decided to make big changes in their lives—like going back to school or moving to another part of the country—how would you respond? Why?

How do you think they might respond if you made a decision like that?

How would remembering God's policy to "forgive and forget" influence your response to somebody who let you down and then tried to make it right?

Let's Listen

Psalm 40   Jonah 3   Acts 9: 1-31

Ephesians 4   1 John 2

Let's Cook

A menu for the new year should include some traditional favorites that reflect your region or your heritage. Add these familiar dishes to the new ideas here, and everybody is sure to remember the food and fun long after they've forgotten the scores of those "can't miss" games.

Slow Roasted Champagne Pot Roast

Serves: 6 | Prep Time: 15 Minutes | Cooking Time: 60 Minutes

Ingredients:

2 lbs.	roast or top sirloin
4 Tbs.	olive oil
1 tsp.	black pepper
2 C	leftover champagne (or substitute a white wine)
½ C	soy sauce
¼ tsp.	salt
3 cloves	garlic, finely chopped
2	bay leaves
6	potatoes, peeled and cut into quarters
6	carrots, chopped into 2 inch sections
3	onions, chopped into quarters
1½ Tbs.	cornstarch
1 Tbs.	warm water (to mix with cornstarch)

Instructions:

Preheat oven to 375 degrees. Season roast with salt and pepper. Heat olive oil on high in large pan. Carefully place meat in pan and sear for 2-3 minutes on each side, creating a "grilled" look. Remove the roast and place in a deep baking dish.

In the same large pan, add the garlic, potatoes, onions, and carrots. Cook for 2-3 minutes, stirring the mixture every now and then. Add champagne, soy sauce, and bay leaves and cook for 1-2 minutes. Add salt and pepper to the liquid according to your taste.

Pour mixture over roast and cover dish with aluminum foil. Use a fork to poke a few small holes for steam to escape. Cook for 45 minutes to 1 hour, or until temperature of meat reaches 140 degrees.

After roast is cooked, let rest for 3-5 minutes before cutting. Place roast in center of large plate, placing the vegetables around it (removing the bay leaves).

To thicken the sauce for gravy, strain the liquid into a saucepan. In a separate bowl, add 1½ tablespoons of cornstarch mixed with 1 tablespoon of water to create a thick, paste-like substance. Add to the sauce and stir attentively until thick.

Roasted Broccoli Spears

Serves: 6 | Prep Time: 10 Minutes | Cooking Time: 10 Minutes

Ingredients:
4 C   water
2 C   broccoli florets, cut into
          3-4 equal pieces
1 C   seasoned bread crumbs
3 Tbs.   olive oil
2 cloves   garlic, finely chopped
¼ tsp.   red pepper flakes
½ tsp.   salt and pepper

Instructions:
Preheat oven to 450 degrees. Fill pot or deep pan with water and bring to a boil. Add broccoli and cook until it turns bright green. Drain water and add olive oil, garlic, salt, pepper, and pepper flakes. Stir the broccoli so that all sides are coated with the olive oil. Remove from pot and place on a cookie sheet. Coat broccoli with breadcrumbs.

Place baking sheet in oven (uncovered) for 7–10 minutes or until you see breadcrumbs darken.

The celebration of the new year should start off with prayer. Putting our best foot forward requires first folding our hands in prayer!

After their audience with [King Herod], [the Magi] set out. And behold, the star that they had seen at its rising preceded them, until it came and stopped over the place where the child was. They were overjoyed at seeing the star, and on entering the house they saw the child with Mary his mother. They prostrated themselves and did him homage. Then they opened their treasures and offered Him gifts of gold, frankincense, and myrrh. And having been warned in a dream not to return to Herod, they departed for their country by another way.

MATTHEW 2: 9-12

Does your family history have a story about a package that was received after the Christmas celebration was over? Maybe it was a box that got accidentally pushed under the sofa or the skirt of the tree. Maybe it was something that Mom saw during the year and put away but then forgot when the holidays finally arrived. Maybe it was a gift from someone far away that arrived long after it was supposed to because it got lost in the mail. Or maybe it was a gift nobody knew about that was discovered among a loved one's possessions after his or her passing. No matter what the reason, a late gift takes on special significance because it stands apart and represents the care the giver took in finding something they hoped would be just right.

That's especially true of the gifts the Magi brought to Jesus, even though they must have seemed very odd to the shepherds who had also made their way to that most holy of places, the manger where the infant Jesus lay. But Scripture tells us that no one rejected the gold, frankincense, and myrrh. Somehow, everyone gathered at the stable where Mary and Joseph had found shelter knew that this was no ordinary birth and no ordinary baby; those extraordinary gifts were, in fact, just right.

Each of those gift-givers experienced supernatural clarity. No wonder they all knelt down. They were in the presence of the King, and they knew it, for God had revealed what they surely would have missed. God had also guided their choice of gifts, just as surely as He had directed their search for Jesus, and protected them by instructing them not to return to King Herod. The Magi's revelation of the Christ Child is called Epiphany. In our language, the word "epiphany" means a moment of sudden understanding or realization. Most moments of realization pale in comparison to the first Epiphany, but it helps to identify with the feeling that comes when we get past a single event and grasp the big picture.

Most of us will never experience a miraculous epiphany like the Magi had, but God has a gift like the one He gave them, prepared for each of His children. That gift is wisdom. The wisdom that God gives is so valuable that when God asked Solomon what he wanted more than anything, Solomon passed up riches and power and requested wisdom, so that he could be a good leader. God responded by giving Solomon great wisdom and the wealth he did not covet.

Wisdom is the very opposite of self-reliance. It comes when we acknowledge that, like the Magi, we need guidance. As parents, we must look ahead

Wisdom comes when we acknowledge we need guidance.

and anticipate God shaping our children and maturing them for His purposes. We need to look for the virtuous qualities they possess that can be encouraged and developed. Parents also need to remember that they weren't left out when the presents were distributed. God has the gift of wisdom for everyone who asks for it. He guarantees the fit because it's exactly what He picked out for each of us. Go ahead and unwrap it!

Jesus was given gold because He was a King, frankincense because He was a Priest, and myrrh because He is the sacrificial Lamb of God who takes away sins.

Let's Talk

Did you ever receive a "late" gift? Why do you remember it?

Did you ever get a gift that you didn't think you'd like or use,

but it surprised you once you gave it a try? What was it?

Have you ever received something that seemed wonderful but turned out to be a big disappointment?

Why didn't it measure up?

If you could request any gift, no matter how big or expensive or

hard to obtain, what would you want? Why?

Do you think that people are only wise in their old age? Who is the wisest person you know?

What good would wisdom do you? When do you think it might be most useful?

If you could give each of your family members a special gift that would last them for a lifetime,

what would you choose? How do you think the recipients would respond?

Let's Listen

I Kings 3   Job 28   Proverbs 4

James 1:17   I Corinthians 1:4-9

Let's Cook

One way to include others in your kitchen conversation about God's storehouse of good things is to invite family and friends to your home and prepare a meal that's unexpectedly festive.

This sauce can be used on any seafood. Mix it with lump crabmeat for crab imperial— a Maryland favorite!

Imperial Salmon

Serves: 6 | Prep Time: 10 Minutes | Cooking Time: 15 Minutes

Ingredients:

6	salmon fillets
½ Tbs.	olive oil
1 C	mayonnaise
¼ C	mustard
2 Tbs.	soy sauce
1 tsp.	Old Bay® Seasoning (or 5 Chinese Spice)
½ tsp.	salt
½ tsp.	pepper
2 tsp.	fresh chopped dill (optional)

Instructions:

Preheat oven to 375 degrees. Season salmon with salt and pepper on fleshy side of the fillet. Heat olive oil in a nonstick pan. Place salmon in pan, skin side down, for 30 seconds to 1 minute. Flip it over and sear the other side for 2-3 minutes. (FYI: While searing the flesh side, you can easily scrape off the seared skin with flat tongs, a fork, or butter knife.) Remove salmon and let rest on a baking sheet.

In a separate bowl, mix together mayonnaise, mustard, soy sauce, and Old Bay® Seasoning, creating a creamy sauce. Use a spatula or spoon to spread the sauce evenly, covering each of the salmon fillets. Place the baking pan uncovered in oven for 10-15 minutes, or until the sauce turns a deep golden brown.

Cheesy Squash

Serves: 6 | Prep Time: 10 Minutes | Cooking Time: 15 Minutes

Ingredients:

3	medium sized yellow squash, cut into ¼ inch fillets
3	medium sized zucchini, cut into ½ inch fillets
4 Tbs.	butter
½ C	olive oil
½ C	Parmesan cheese, freshly grated
½ tsp.	salt and pepper
1 tsp.	dried oregano

Instructions:

Preheat oven to 400 degrees. Place veggie "fillets" on a baking sheet. Melt butter, olive oil, and oregano together in saucepan or in a microwave. Stir together and pour over the vegetables and mix all together so that each fillet is coated with the mix. Shake salt and pepper over all of the vegetables—both sides. Place in oven for 10-15 minutes. After vegetables are cooked, remove from the oven and shake or shave fresh Parmesan cheese over them at the last minute. Serve this one hot!

Celebrating the Epiphany can remind us that Christmas doesn't last one day, but every time we celebrate God's gifts to us!

CHAPTER 3
Soups and Smiles
SUGGESTED FOR WORLD DAY OF THE SICK

Then the righteous will answer him and say, "Lord, when did we see you hungry and feed you, or thirsty and give you drink? When did we see you a stranger and welcome you, or naked and clothe you? When did we see you ill or in prison, and visit you?" And the king will say to them in reply, "Amen, I say to you, whatever you did for one of these least brothers of mine, you did for me."

MATTHEW 25: 37-40

Old-fashioned meatloaf. Homemade macaroni and cheese. Grandma's chocolate chip cookies. We have a name for dishes that remind us of our childhood or make us feel safe at home after a tough day out in the world. We call them comfort foods. It's a good term, but it's not quite so good a concept. The problem? It's all about us.

Comfort is not a do-it-yourself project. It's a do-for-others way of living that comes back to us in unexpected ways that feel better than pampering ourselves ever could. This idea runs counter to what we see in our magazines and hear on our televisions. It is not the message our sons and daughters are hearing. Taking care of others is such an alien concept in our self-centered world that it is crucial for us to show and tell our children the truth: "Looking out for number one" is not their responsibility—it's God's. God, in His perfect Wisdom, gives us the responsibility to bring kindness to others.

Not everyone is called to a religous vocational ministry, but all of us, no matter our age or our circumstances, are called to pass on the love of Christ by caring for the people around us. Jesus could not have spoken more plainly on the subject. If we love Christ, we cannot ignore the suffering of those around us. Mother Teresa said that when she looked into the eyes of the suffering, she saw Jesus. Her example should inspire us to look beyond ourselves for the people God puts on our path.

> *If we love Christ, we cannot ignore the suffering of those around us.*

You may be thinking to yourself that it was easy for Mother Teresa to find the needy in Calcutta, but where are the people your family can help? They might be as close as the elderly couple next door, the single mom you see in the after-school pick-up lane, or the family in your church with a child who has special needs. It could be a coworker who is recovering from an accident or the new family who just moved from across the country and doesn't have relatives nearby. It might be someone within your own family—a grandparent who puts up a self-sufficient front but has fewer friends and outside activities these days. There is someone. How do we know? God would not tell us to do something we cannot do. And what does it mean to show kindness? The answer to that question is laid out for us, too. We call it the Golden Rule. Kindness is giving others what we would want them to give us. And still better, to love as God loved us.

What would feel like kindness to you? The answers are endless. Look at the person you are about to serve; put yourself in his or her place. If you were new in town, wouldn't you welcome a basket with a homemade meal and a small gift, like a local coupon book or the names and numbers of the neighbors along with an invitation to an upcoming get-together? If you were responsible for a child who required round-the-clock care, wouldn't you welcome a gift of fresh baked goods and the offer to run an errand or help out with home care so you could have a respite? If you were lonely, wouldn't you be pleased with unexpected visitors bearing the ingredients for an impromptu meal to share?

Your child may surprise you with his or her awareness of others' needs and willingness to care for them. Kids tend to speak candidly with friends and classmates and reveal situations that adults often struggle with alone. As you deliberately act out of kindness, remember that God is not only using you as His ambassador, He is using you to shape the character of your child and preparing both of you for future blessings. Trust His plan. Let Him take care of you and your family's needs while you make some hearty soup and deliver it with some crisp crackers and a big smile.

World Day of the Sick is generally on February 11, the feast of Our Lady of Lourdes, a shrine in France where countless miraculous healings have taken place.

Let's Talk

Think of the advertisements you've seen lately.

Which ones tell you that you deserve the product they're selling?

When you don't feel good, what makes you more comfortable?

When you visit someone in a hospital or nursing home, how do you feel?

What would make you feel more at ease?

If you faced a crisis, where would you look for help?

Why do you think some people don't pay attention when they see

a person who is obviously living on the streets?

How does it make you feel when you do something nice for someone who can't return the favor?

Let's Listen

2 Kings 4   Psalm 69   Isaiah 58   Acts 20

Let's Cook

ARROZ CALDO SOUP
GRILLED CREAMY VEGETABLE SOUP
SIMPLE FRENCH ONION SOUP

These soup recipes provide you with a chance to help a friend in need. Your goal is to present them with healthful, tasty food in a way that demonstrates caring and thoughtfulness, not duty. When you deliver the meal, allow enough time in your schedule so you can freshen the glass of water at the bedside or do some light cleaning before you go. Your small acts will mean more than you ever expected.

> *To facilitate the cooking and reheating process, keep garnish (such as croutons, sour cream, chives, and cheese) in separate containers.*

Arroz Caldo—Hot Rice, Chicken and Ginger Soup

Serves: 4 | Prep Time: 10 Minutes | Cooking Time: 20 Minutes

Ingredients:

1 C	rice
2	chicken breasts, cut into ½ inch cubes
3 tsp.	fresh ginger, grated
1	medium onion, finely chopped
1 Tbs.	vegetable oil
2 cloves	garlic, minced
1 tsp.	salt
1 tsp.	black pepper
2	scallions, minced
7–10 C	boiling water (depending on how creamy you want your soup)
	Tabasco® sauce (optional)

Instructions:

Cut chicken into cubes and season with salt and pepper. Heat oil in a large saucepan. Add ginger and garlic. Sauté. Immediately add chicken and brown on all sides. Add onions and continue to cook until onions become clear.

Add rice to the mixture and cook until rice becomes slightly colored. Add hot water one cup at a time so that the rice becomes creamy. This usually takes about 2-3 minutes. Continue to add water, and continue to stir. Salt and pepper to taste.

When rice is soft, the soup is cooked. The soup is generally served very thick, almost like porridge. To thin it out, just add a cup or two of hot water and be sure to season accordingly. Serve with a few splashes of Tabasco® sauce and a sprinkle of scallions for garnish and extra flavoring.

Grilled Creamy Vegetable Soup

Serves: 4 | Prep Time: 15 Minutes | Cooking Time: 20 Minutes

Ingredients:

1 C	carrots, chopped into ½ inch pieces
1 C	broccoli flowers, chopped in half
1 C	zucchini, chopped into ¼ inch pieces
1 C	fresh tomatoes, chopped into ¼ inch pieces
1	medium white onion, minced
½ tsp.	salt
¼ tsp.	pepper
1 tsp.	oregano
1 clove	garlic, finely minced
3 Tbs.	olive oil
3 C	chicken or beef broth
1 C	whipping cream
2 Tbs.	butter
1 Tbs.	flour
2 C	croutons
4 tsp.	sour cream
1 Tbs.	chives, chopped (for garnish)

Instructions:

Turn oven to broil. Place chopped vegetables onto a cookie sheet and season with olive oil, salt, pepper, and oregano. Place veggies on middle rack of broiler for approx. 10 minutes, or until caramelizing occurs. Remove and cook the other side of the veggies for 3-5 minutes.

Remove and place the vegetables and the natural juices in a food processor or blender. Use some of the broth to help the blending process. (If using a blender, you may be required to repeat this process a few times so as to not overload the blender.) In a pot over medium heat, melt butter and add flour, creating a roux. Add one cup of broth, stirring to thicken the roux and avoiding lumps. Add the pureed vegetables. Continue to add one cup of stock at a time, while mixing and tasting for consistency. Add whipping cream and continue to stir. Salt and pepper to taste. Drop heat to low, allowing flavors to simmer together for about 5 minutes.

Ladle into bowls and dollop with a teaspoon of sour cream in each bowl. Evenly distribute croutons around the sour cream and drop a pinch or two of the chopped chives for garnish.

Simple French Onion Soup

Serves: 4 | Prep Time: 10 Minutes | Cooking Time: 15 Minutes

Ingredients:

3	medium-sized white onions, sliced in ¼ inch rings
2 Tbs.	butter
1 qt.	beef or chicken broth
3 Tbs.	Sherry wine (optional)
1 tsp.	Worcestershire sauce
1 tsp.	salt
½ tsp.	pepper
4 slices	provolone cheese
2 C	croutons

Instructions:

Preheat oven to 350 degrees. Melt butter in pot and add onions to sauté. Cook until limp. Add broth, sherry, and Worcestershire sauce. Bring to light boil. Add salt and pepper. Distribute broth and onions into four individual oven-safe bowls or four extra-large mugs. Fill each bowl ¾ full.

Top each bowl with ½ cup of croutons and place one slice of cheese over each bowl. Place bowls on top of a cookie sheet and put in oven for 7-10 minutes or until cheese begins to bubble or melt.

CHAPTER 4
Adjusting Focus
SUGGESTED FOR ASH WEDNESDAY

Filled with the holy Spirit, Jesus returned from the Jordan and was led by the Spirit into the desert for forty days, to be tempted by the devil. He ate nothing during those days, and when they were over he was hungry. The devil said to him, "If you are the Son of God, command this stone to become bread." Jesus answered him, "It is written, 'One does not live by bread alone.'" Then he took him up and showed him all the kingdoms of the world in a single instant. The devil said to him, "I shall give to you all this power and their glory; for it has been handed over to me, and I may give it to whomever I wish. All this will be yours, if you worship me." Jesus said to him in reply, "It is written: 'You shall worship the Lord, your God, and him alone shall you serve.'"

LUKE 4: 1-8

"It's a matter of perspective." How many times have you heard that when people are discussing a topic that's generating a range of opinions? The music of your youth was incessant noise to your parents. The out-of-style clothes you shoved to the back of your closet are the retro styles your teen prefers. The art you just don't get sets an auction record, leaving you to wonder if you can teach the dog to hold a paint brush and create a similar "masterpiece."

19

Perspective has everything to do with how you and your family approach Ash Wednesday and the forty days of Lent. In some ways it seems like a long time between candy bars or T-bones or whatever it is you've decided to do without. That's the part that comedians play up when they joke about what people give up for Lent.

Lent certainly is a time to remember what Jesus went through during His forty days in the desert. He not only fasted, He withstood Satan's challenges and taunting. We might be able to convince ourselves we're suffering when we observe Lent, but we know we will never come close to what Jesus endured.

So how can we make the most of Lent and use this time for the good of our family and our faith? If we shift perspectives, we might be

Life is more than the accumulation of things. There is so much to gain when we opt for less.

surprised by what we can gain in just forty days. Surely we will be ready to celebrate the joy of Easter with new enthusiasm.

How can that be? Simplifying gives us time to pay attention to the essentials. Making a homemade soup instead of a roast allows us more time to share the day as we chop the celery or slice the potatoes that go into our family recipe. Spending less per serving with a meatless meal makes it easier to invite friends to stay for dinner. Shopping less saves time that can be used for conversations about whether your family might be happier if you had less, instead of putting all your energy into accumulating more.

These aren't questions with right or wrong answers, and it is likely that the conversations will go on for some time as you consider all that you have to be thankful for and how you might use your blessings for the good of others. Don't be afraid to raise these issues with your children. Even when they're pushing you for the latest sneakers and CDs, they know they live comfortable lives. Help them to understand that success in life is much more than the accumulation of things by showing them what they can gain when they opt for less.

A shift in perspective can help us make the most of the Lenten season.

Let's Talk

Think about a time when you were really hungry. How did you feel?
Have you ever thought about what it would be like not to have food for weeks?

Sometimes people fast as part of a religious observance.
Why do you think they do that? What do they gain?

During his forty days in the desert, Jesus was tempted again and again, just like you.
How do you resist temptation?

If you and your family decided to change your lifestyle, what would you be willing to give up?
What would you definitely want to keep?

Have you ever done something nice for someone else and been surprised by
how good your kindness made you feel?

Lent only lasts forty days. What aspect of this observance
would you like to make a part of your whole year?

Let's Listen

Psalm 4   Jonah 2   Matthew 12   1 John 4

Let's Cook

The tradition of abstaining from meat products during Lent reminds us of the staple of food in Jesus' time: fish. In fact, the Greek phrase "Jesus Christ Is Lord" creates the acronym "FISH" in that language. Eating fish is a reminder of Jesus!

> *Al dente is an Italian expression for how pasta is cooked. It means "to the tooth." The pasta should be taken off the stove while it is still slightly firm.*

Meatless certainly doesn't have to mean tasteless. There are lots of vegetarian and meatless recipes your family will want all year round, but we think this menu will become a favorite.

Spaghetti Aglio e Olio
(Spaghetti with Olive Oil and Garlic)

Serves: 4 | Prep Time: 10 Minutes | Cooking Time: 15 Minutes

Ingredients:

1 box	thick spaghetti
4 Tbs.	olive oil
2 Tbs.	parsley, freshly chopped (flat Italian parsely preferred)
2 cloves	garlic, thinly sliced
2 pinches	red pepper flakes
1	anchovy fillet, mashed with a fork (optional)
¾ tsp.	salt
¼ tsp.	black pepper
½ C	fresh Parmesan cheese

Instructions:

Boil spaghetti until al dente (almost cooked but still a bit firm). Drain the pasta, but save about 2-3 tablespoons of the hot pasta water.

Heat oil in a pan, and when hot, add the anchovy fillet and assist the breaking up process with a wooden spoon or fork. Add the garlic and red pepper flakes (this process takes only 2-3 minutes maximum—you don't want to burn the garlic, so monitor the timing between the pasta and heating up the oil).

Carefully add the hot olive oil mixture to the pot and stir ingredients together. Add salt and pepper. Add the freshly chopped parley and Parmesan cheese and mix together. Serve on individual plates, adding grated Parmesan cheese according to taste.

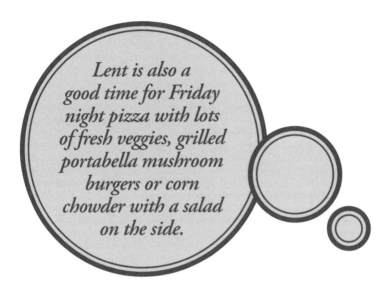

Lent is also a good time for Friday night pizza with lots of fresh veggies, grilled portabella mushroom burgers or corn chowder with a salad on the side.

Caprese Salad

Serves: 4 | Prep Time: 10 Minutes

Ingredients:

2 balls	fresh, water-packed mozzarella cheese
2	large tomatoes
8	fresh basil leaves, minced
4 Tbs.	extra virgin olive oil
1 Tbs.	balsamic vinegar
½ tsp.	salt
¼ tsp.	pepper

Instructions:

Cut each tomato and each piece of mozzarella into 4 equal rings. Place two rings of tomato on each plate, and then top each off with a slice of cheese. Sprinkle on some of the freshly minced basil (or 2 light dashes of dried basil). Add salt and pepper on each of the individual tomato and cheese rings. Mix the olive oil and vinegar together and spoon about 1 tablespoon of the mixture over each.

CHAPTER 5
Why Sacrifice?
SUGGESTED FOR THE FRIDAYS OF LENT

Rid yourselves of all malice and all deceit, insincerity, envy, and all slander; like newborn infants, long for pure spiritual milk so that through it you may grow into salvation, for you have tasted that the Lord is good. Come to him, a living stone, rejected by human beings but chosen and precious in the sight of God, and, like living stones, let yourselves be built into a spiritual house to be a holy priesthood to offer spiritual sacrifices acceptable to God through Jesus Christ.

1 PETER 2: 1-5

From the beginning of human history, God has instructed His people through the practice of sacrifice. It started when Cain and Abel, the sons of Adam, brought offerings to the Lord. Abel brought the best that he had, his first-born animals. Cain brought what was easy for him to part with from his garden. The Bible says God accepted Abel's gift but looked with disfavor on Cain's. Cain did not hide his anger, and God warned him not to let evil get the best of him. We know that Cain ignored that warning. In contrast, Abraham trusted God even when he thought the sacrifice God required was his son, Isaac. When God saw Abraham's obedience, He blessed Abraham, first by sparing Isaac's life and providing a ram for the sacrifice, then by promising Abraham that his descendents would be a blessing to all the earth.

God does not ask us to sacrifice because He needs something from us. Instead, He wants us to understand the enormity of His love for us. Sacrifice is not about money. It is about everything. It is the willingness to give up your evening of relaxation to sit in a hospital waiting room with a neighbor whose husband has just had a heart attack. It is the decision to drive the old car for another year and put the extra money into a fund for your church's mission to orphans in Haiti. It is the willingness to visit your elderly aunt and assure her of your love even though she no longer remembers your name and may not remember your visit an hour after you've gone. Sacrifice is being alert to what God asks of you, and then doing it with confidence in His good plan.

> *Every Friday in Lent is a mini-commemoration of Good Friday. TGIF can have an entirely different meaning if we remember why Fridays are so important.*

Your sons and daughters need help to understand the power and the price of sacrifice. They may resist the idea of doing without unless they see the purpose behind it. But when teens understand that willing sacrifices please God and bless others, they will be drawn into the circle of expectancy that faith creates as they watch their sacrifices be converted into someone else's smile.

During Lent, the practice of eating sacrificially on Fridays naturally encourages a family tradition of serving sacrificially on those days, too. Where could you give your time? Is there a project you could take on for an elderly neighbor or relative? Is there a family who would be encouraged by sharing your simple Friday meal? Do you have clothes you could share with a family whose children are outgrowing their budget? Can you give up tickets to that Friday game so a single mom can treat her kids to something she could not afford to give them herself?

Your sacrifices, big and small, during your observance of Lent will return to you and your family as new blessings when you consider the cost of Good Friday and the wonder of Easter.

Sacrifice is about more than money. It is about being alert to what God asks of you, and then doing it with confidence in His good plan.

Let's Talk

There's a famous Texas putdown: "All hat but no cattle."

How do you think that idea might apply to attitudes and acts of sacrifice?

What does it mean to live sacrificially?

Think about sacrifices that go beyond food and money.

Why do you think God is offended by some "sacrifices"?

What do you treasure? How could it be used sacrificially?

Have you ever considered the cost of God's sacrifice for you?

Why did He do that?

How would you explain what it means to sacrifice to a small child?

Let's Listen

Genesis 22   I Samuel 15: 13-30   Mark 12: 28-34   Romans 12

Let's Cook

OPEN-FACED TUNA MUFFIN
WITH SIMPLE FESTIVE SALAD

Identifying with those in need can teach us a lot. In many parts of the world, as well as many homes in our country, foods we think of as staples are luxuries. As you take the time to put together a "frugal" meal, God will give you creative ideas for making this sacrifice a truly special time of worship in word and deed.

> *Meals on Lenten Fridays should be more than cheese pizzas. They should be about creating flavors from simple ingredients.*

Open Faced Tuna Muffin with Sautéed Mushrooms

Serves: 3 | Prep Time: 10 Minutes | Cooking Time: 10 Minutes

Ingredients:

3	English muffins
2	6 oz. cans chunky tuna, drained
2 Tbs.	mayonnaise
1 Tbs.	sour cream
1 stalk	celery, chopped into ¼ inch pieces
6 slices	provolone cheese
¼ tsp.	paprika
1 clove	garlic, minced
2 C	button mushrooms, chopped
1 Tbs.	butter
½ tsp.	salt
¼ tsp.	pepper
¼ tsp.	fresh parsley

Instructions:

Preheat oven to 350 degrees. Separate the English muffins and place face side up on a baking pan.

Melt ½ tablespoon of butter in a saucepan and sauté the mushrooms. Remove mushrooms and set aside in a bowl. In the same saucepan, melt the other ½ tablespoon of butter and add the tuna, mayonnaise, sour cream, celery, salt, pepper, and paprika. Mix well over medium heat for 2-4 minutes.

Assemble the open-faced sandwiches by layering mushrooms on the English muffins and topping with about 2 tablespoons of the tuna mix. Place a slice of provolone cheese on top of each. Sprinkle parsley over the open-faced muffins. Put in oven for 8-10 minutes or until cheese is melted.

Simple Festive Salad

Serves: 3 | Prep Time: 10 Minutes

Ingredients:

1 bag	pre-washed mixed field greens
2	tomatoes, cut into wedges
2 Tbs.	lemon juice
¼ C	extra virgin olive oil
¼ C	feta or bleu cheese
¼ C	walnuts
2-4 pinches	salt and pepper
½ C	dried cranberries

Instructions:

Lightly sprinkle mixed field greens and tomato wedges with salt and pepper. Whisk together the oil and lemon juice. Add the bleu cheese, walnuts, and cranberries. Mix together and pour over the salad. Toss salad and add more salt and pepper to taste if necessary. When plating, be sure to continue to toss the salad, as the flavored ingredients tend to make their way to the bottom of the bowl.

This is a good time to remember what matters most about our meals is not what's on our plates, but what's in our hearts as we cook and serve and share.

CHAPTER 6
Good Job!
RITES OF PASSAGE

His master said to him, "Well done, my good and faithful servant.

Since you were faithful in small matters, I will give you great responsibilities.

Come, share your master's joy."

MATTHEW 25:23

"You're my mother—you have to say that." Those all-too-familiar words are repeated every day by millions of kids who are worried about their looks, or their ability to play on the varsity team, or the likelihood that they'll have a date for the prom, or any of a hundred other challenges that make the middle school and high school years tough to navigate.

When their self-assessments are skewed toward "loser," teens don't quite know how to respond to a parental word of praise or encouragement that counters their critical evaluation. In their minds, anything positive has to be fiction. That's why a parent's attempt to help may be wrongly interpreted as pity or the expectation of failure.

There is, however, a way for parents to assure children of their confidence in them. The solution is so simple and obvious it is easy to overlook: Celebrate, Celebrate, Celebrate! Use every opportunity you can find to specifically tell your teen what is going right. This might take some getting used to because parents are more habituated to spotting the undone than the done, but the effort will pay off.

Find something to praise every day and point it out. Start the day with a casual remark like, "I think that shirt looks good on you," or "I'm looking forward to getting to your game this afternoon." Individually, these remarks don't carry much weight, but cumulatively they convey that you are paying attention to your teen, and you like what you see. Bit by bit, these positive messages wear away negative self-perception and build a sense of worth.

Use the student council campaign, the learner's permit, the appreciative thanks from the

Both milestones and everyday events can be cause for a little celebration and a lot of affirmation.

neighbor whose lawn got mowed, the first driver's license, the completed term paper, the science fair project that made it to school in one piece, or success in a game or on the stage as a reason to add a dessert to dinner or make a favorite meal. Every time you take note of a life mile-marker or a sign of progress and maturity, you are inoculating your son or daughter against the moments of despair that often make him or her deaf to the very same message. Accenting the positive at a moment when there is tangible proof of accomplishment provides an argument-free situation in which parents and other family members can express their pride, first in the child and then in the accomplishment.

You're not independently saying you think your daughter will make a good driver, you're repeating the opinion of the examiner who handed out the passing test grade. You're not exaggerating your son's intelligence, you're happily noting where he landed in the national percentile for students who also took that achievement test. You're not insisting that you gave birth to a future

> *Let your kids know you're willing to settle for less drama in exchange for a sincere hug.*

Academy Award winner, you're saying that you will be an enthusiastic part of the audience on opening night at the school play.

As you work together to make a special just-for-us family meal, consider the possibility that you are creating a tradition that your children and their future spouses will use to mark their children's successes. Your grandchildren will always know what you are telling your children now: Their very existence, not their accomplishments, is a reason to have a party every day.

Let's Talk

Did your grade school teacher use gold stars? How did it feel to get one?

How did it feel when you didn't get one?

How did you form your opinion of yourself as an athlete?

What could change that opinion?

Some youth sports leagues give trophies to everybody on every team, while others limit awards
to their champions and stars. Which approach do you think is most helpful to players? Why?

Look at your friends' families.

Do you see contrasting ways of handling accomplishments and challenges?

Have you ever helped a small child perfect a skill like walking or learning the alphabet?
How did you encourage him or her to keep trying when the going got tough?

If celebration suppers become regular events at your house,

what do you want to celebrate next?

Let's Listen

Zephaniah 3: 14-20   Matthew 25: 14-30   Luke 15: 11-32   2 Corinthians 8

Let's Cook

POACHED SALMON TOPPED
WITH CREAMED ASPARAGUS DRESSING

"This calls for a celebration" can become one of your family's favorite expressions when you decide together that you aren't going to let each other's accomplishments, both tiny and terrific, slip by unnoticed. This menu expresses your willingness to do something extra on those special occasions.

Poached Salmon and Creamed Asparagus Dressing

Serves: 6 | Prep Time: 15 Minutes | Cooking Time: 20 Minutes

Poached Salmon

Ingredients:

6	individual portion salmon fillets
3 Tbs.	olive oil
2 C	orange juice
1 C	white wine
3 Tbs.	honey or syrup
1 tsp.	salt
½ tsp.	black pepper
2	bay leaves
2 cloves	garlic, thinly sliced

Instructions:

Salt and pepper salmon on both sides. In a deep pan, add olive oil, orange juice, wine, honey or syrup, bay leaves, and garlic slices. Cook over medium heat until liquids begin to simmer. Add salmon and poach for 5-7 minutes on each side uncovered.

Remove salmon and let rest away from the liquids. Continue to cook liquids until reduced by half. The thick liquid, after straining, serves as a nice saucy base on which to place the salmon.

Dressing

Ingredients:

10-15	fresh asparagus stalks
1½ C	sour cream
	Fresh dill (for garnish)

Instructions:

Prepare asparagus by cutting or breaking off the woody part of the stems. In a deep-dish pan, add hot water and let it come to a boil. Add asparagus and cook until it turns bright green and tender (not too soft).

Remove asparagus immediately and place in a food processor with 1½ - 2 cups of sour cream. Salt and pepper to taste (approximately ½ teaspoon of salt and ¼ teaspoon of black pepper) and blend to a creamy light green consistency. Use a serving spoon to top off the poached salmon with dressing. Garnish with sprig of dill.

Parents like to have their accomplishments celebrated as much as kids do. Don't leave them out of the fun!

CHAPTER 7
Heat and Light
SUGGESTED FOR PENTECOST SUNDAY

When the time for Pentecost was fulfilled, they were all in one place together…

And they were all filled with the Holy Spirit and began to speak in different tongues,

as the Spirit enabled them to proclaim.

ACTS 2: 1-4

What kind of power could change a small group of frightened and confused men and women into fearless witnesses for their faith? The same kind that is available to you and every believer today. Christ Himself promised that power when He commissioned the 72 who went before Him to proclaim the Good News of salvation. He promised that power again after the resurrection, when He told His disciples to stay in the city until He sent what the Father had promised, so that they would be "clothed with power from on high."

That power arrived on Pentecost, and ever since that day, the presence or indwelling of God Himself, in the person of the Holy Spirit, comes to everyone who becomes a new creature in Christ. The Apostle Paul tells us in his letter to Rome that apart from Christ, we are dead in our sin. But God regenerates us and gives us a new heart when He draws us to Christ. Paul calls this the "free gift of God." Regeneration is the work of the Holy Spirit, who takes up residence in that new heart, making a new life possible. Every believer has been touched by the Holy Spirit.

Every believer depends on the Holy Spirit for the power to live a life that reflects Christ and rejects evil.

In their new lives, the disciples were radically changed. They were empowered by the Holy Spirit to follow Christ's commission to go out into the world and proclaim God's truth. They were able to speak in languages they had never learned and be easily understood by the people around them. They were able to preach boldly, even when threatened with death, and they were able to live in a way that amazed people and made them want that same power.

> *Every believer depends on the Holy Spirit for the power to live a life that reflects Christ and rejects evil.*

The cynics of the day accused the disciples of drunkenness, but the Apostle Peter boldly corrected them. Because of the power of the Holy Spirit, Peter was a changed man, no longer afraid to be publicly identified as a follower of Christ. He now welcomed the opportunity to address the thousands who gathered. Peter reminded the doubters in the crowd that it was morning; no one had been drinking. What they were witnessing was the fulfillment of Joel's prophesy that "God would pour out His Spirit on His people; He would fill them with His presence." Peter told the crowd that Jesus Christ was alive and that He was both Lord and Christ. His audience listened, wanting to know what they should do. Without hesitation, Peter told them to repent and be baptized so they, too, could receive new life and the presence of the Holy Spirit. Peter said that God's promises were for all those He called to Himself. Peter's message got through. That day, 3,000 people were moved from spiritual death to life. As the disciples and the growing band of new believers continued to share their faith, their numbers increased daily.

Now we are a part of that band of believers. We are in that line that stretches from the first Pentecost to today. On this very day, new believers will be called to Christ by the power of the Holy Spirit. It is the Spirit who empowers us, all of us, to share our faith. The Holy Spirit provides security at moments when we would otherwise be afraid. He gives peace when our human impulse is to panic. He provides boldness when we would be timid. The Holy Spirit is the fire that melts our icy hearts. He is the light that finds us and leads us when we cannot see. He is our perfect comfort when we ache. The Holy Spirit is the embodiment of Christ's promise that He would never leave or forsake those He redeemed.

Has your faith been a little flat? Ask the Holy Spirit to fill you with His presence. Do you worry about the challenges of life, especially the surprises of parenting? Ask the Holy Spirit for confidence. Are there people you love who are cold toward faith? Ask the Holy Spirit to give you the boldness the disciples had on Pentecost. Go ahead and ask. The presence of the Holy Spirit is not restricted to others. It is your birthright as a believer and your gift from on high.

> *Do you worry about the challenges of life, especially the surprises of parenting? Ask the Holy Spirit for confidence.*

Let's Talk

Why do you think Jesus promised the Holy Spirit to believers?

Do you feel believers in the twenty-first century can understand what Pentecost was like? Why or why not?

Some people use the term Holy Ghost when referring to the Holy Spirit. How would you help a child understand this term?

Does your family history include someone like the Apostle Peter or the Apostle Paul whose life was turned around by faith and the power of the Holy Spirit?

If you were to ask the Holy Spirit for one thing today, what would it be?

When you think about having conversations with unbelievers, does the Holy Spirit's promise to supply the words you need make you more comfortable?

Let's Listen

Joel 3   Mark 16   Acts 2

1 Corinthians 14   Hebrews 2

Let's Cook

Pentecost marks the point when the Gospel began spreading to all nations. It's all about energy and enthusiasm and power. A menu to celebrate the arrival of the Holy Spirit should be rich in flavors, even unfamiliar ones. If you have

Try something new! Fusion foods combine various ethnic styles to create surprising and bold flavors.

invited guests to share your meal, ask the Holy Spirit to use the time together as an opportunity for you to talk about your faith and how your life is different because the Holy Spirit is at work in you.

Cola Pork Skewers

Serves: 6 | Prep Time: 3 hours (including marinade) | Cooking Time: 20 Minutes

Ingredients:

12-14	skewers (wooden or metal)
3-4 lb.	pork butt, cut into 1 inch cubes (measure to have 6-7 cubes per skewer)
5 cloves	garlic, chopped
1 Tbs.	salt
½ Tbs.	pepper
1 can	dark cola soda—flat (let out carbonation by pouring can into a glass and letting sit until flat)
½ C	soy sauce
6 Tbs.	ketchup
3	bay leaves
6 Tbs.	olive oil

Instructions:

Season pork with salt and pepper. In a glass or non-reactive bowl, prepare a marinade by mixing together the flat cola, soy sauce, ketchup, bay leaves, and garlic. Add pork to the marinade and cover with plastic wrap. Let sit for at least 3 hours in refrigerator.

Preheat grill when ready to cook. Skewer the meats, adding 6-7 cubes to each skewer. After all the skewers are in place, drizzle a little olive oil over all of them. When grill is ready, place skewers directly over the heat, turning every 3-5 minutes on each side. This dish tastes great with sticky white rice.

Sweet Asian Slaw

Serves: 6 | Prep Time: 35 Minutes

Ingredients:

½ head	cabbage, finely shredded (approximately 6-8 cups)
3	carrots, shredded
2	oranges, peeled and sliced (or 2 small cans of mandarin oranges, drained)
6 Tbs.	soy sauce
6 tsp.	rice wine vinegar (or plain distilled white vinegar)
1 C	mayonnaise
¼ tsp.	hot chili powder
4 Tbs.	fresh cilantro, chopped
4 Tbs.	fresh flat-leaf parsley, chopped
½ tsp.	pepper
½ C	cashews

Instructions:

In a large bowl, add soy sauce, vinegar, mayonnaise, chili powder, cilantro, parsley, and pepper. Whisk together. Toss the cabbage and carrots into the sauce. Cover bowl with plastic wrap and let sit in refrigerator for about 20-30 minutes. Immediately prior to serving, mix in the oranges and cashews to add another level of flavor.

Alternate meal idea: Celebrate by preparing fondue or a flaming dessert to symbolize the fire the Holy Spirit ignites in our lives.

CHAPTER 8
Turning the Table
SUGGESTED FOR MOTHER'S DAY

Her children rise up and praise her; her husband, too, extols her: "Many are the women of proven worth, but you have excelled them all." Charm is deceptive and beauty fleeting; the woman who fears the LORD is to be praised.

PROVERBS 31: 28-30

It's hard to imagine now, but it took an act of Congress in 1914 to make Mother's Day a national celebration. Thanks to all the gentle reminders, flower sales on Mother's Day are double what they are on Valentine's Day. The day is a record setter for long-distance phone carriers, and it generates the sale of 155 million individual greeting cards, a number that doesn't even include those one-of-a-kind construction paper originals. No one keeps statistics on how many Mother's Day cards are tucked away in drawers and scrapbooks, but it would be safe to assume that number is in the billions.

A mother does not expect a lot of attention for her work. She knows it's a round-the-clock assignment that will continue in some form until the day she dies. And if her own mother is no longer living, a mother knows her influence will last beyond her lifetime, just as her own mother's has for her.

A mother's job description often seems to focus on tasks like diaper changing, laundering, chaperoning, providing medical care, monitoring homework, supervising chores, cleaning, shopping, scheduling, waitressing, gift wrapping, caring for pets, and so on and so on.

That's all true, but the real role of a mother is not about tasks. It is about the intangibles of caring in a way that is truly unique. Mothers start loving their children long before they ever see them. They love the very idea of being a mother, and long to hold their child from the moment they know he or she is on the way. This is not simply biology; it is as true of adoptive mothers as it is of mothers who give birth. Children do not grow under their mothers' hearts. They grow in them.

Love is expressed in as many different ways as there are mothers and children. You see it on refrigerator doors where artwork and grade reports are posted for everybody to see. You hear it at soccer games and school concerts where it is easy to determine which fan belongs to which "star." You feel it when you catch the look of a mother as she watches her child during those milestone moments that she helped make possible.

Because a mother's priority is others, she will protest that no one "should make a fuss" for Mother's Day. She will excuse her husband's failure to acknowledge the day by saying she's not his mother, though she will probably purchase a card for him to send his mother. She will understand any reason a child offers for not having time to send a card or make a call. After all, she's Mom, and she always looks for the best in her children, even when no one else can see it.

When we think about how much our mothers love us, one day to celebrate them hardly seems like enough. So even though they will tell you

> *The real role of a mother is about the intangibles of caring in a way that is truly unique.*

not to, make this day as special as you can. Don't worry about spending money. The gifts that mean the most to a mother don't cost a penny. Find a sheet of paper and write a thank-you note. Look around the house and find a project like cleaning out the hall closet or straightening up the family room that you can do without being asked. Offer to take a walk with your mother so you can catch up with each other. Ban her from the kitchen and the laundry room for an entire day, and hand her a book you've checked out of the library for her to enjoy. Think of something she does out of love for you, and do it for her. Don't be surprised if she cries a little. Moms are like that.

Set the tone with a surprise breakfast. Place a note or a prayer card on the tray or by Mom's place at the table.

Let's Talk

What is your favorite thing about your mother?

Does she know that?

What does she do that drives you crazy? Why does it drive you crazy?

Compared to other mothers you know, is your mom more or less strict? Is that a good or bad thing?

What makes your mother laugh?

Do you know what your grandmother was like as a parent?

How do you think she influences your mother?

Solomon demonstrated his wisdom when he settled a dispute between two women who both claimed to be the mother of a baby. He recommended that the child be divided in half. Why?

Which of your mother's traits do you hope to bring to your own parenting?

Let's Listen

Exodus 20:12   Proverbs 31: 10-31   Isaiah 66: 13

John 19:25-27   II Timothy 2: 1-5

Let's Cook

It wouldn't matter if the toast were burnt and the coffee spilled a little, any meal for Mom will be welcomed with a smile. This menu is not overly complicated, so everybody in the family (except Mom!) can help in its preparation and be in on the surprise when it's served. Go ahead and use the good china!

This fancy breakfast sandwich takes a bit of work, but the result is a one-plate meal that includes all the favorite breakfast flavors!

Monte Cristo

Serves: 1 | Prep Time: 10 Minutes | Cooking Time: 15 Minutes

Ingredients:

3 pieces	white bread, crust removed
4 slices	cooked ham
2 thin slices	Brie cheese, casing removed (or sharp provolone cheese slice)
2	eggs, beaten with 2 teaspoons water
1 tsp.	vanilla extract
2 Tbs.	butter
1 C	bread crumbs
	Maple syrup, slightly warmed

Instructions:

Beat together eggs, water, and vanilla extract. Lightly coat both sides of each piece of bread in the egg mixture.

Assemble a simple triple-decker sandwich by placing 2 slices of ham and a thin layer of cheese between each piece of bread. Put sandwich together and cut diagonally to make 2 small triangles.

Dip each triangle of the sandwich on all sides into the batter once again, and coat all sides of sandwich in breadcrumbs. In a nonstick frying pan, melt butter over medium heat and place the sandwich flat on the pan for approximately 1-2 minutes. Do this on each side. The egg batter around the sandwich edges should also be cooked, using tongs to hold the sandwich together while allowing the edges to cook for about 30 seconds on each exposed side. Drizzle with maple syrup warmed in the microwave.

With my mother, Fe,
at my college graduation.

Mother's Day is not a religious celebration, unless you see your mother as a gift from God!

Breakfast Berries

Serves: 1 | Prep Time: 5 Minutes

Ingredients:
- ¼ C   fresh strawberries
- ¼ C   fresh blueberries (or any other fresh berries)
- ½ C   sweetened condensed milk
- ½ C   evaporated milk
- ¼ tsp.   fresh mint leaves, finely minced
- ½ tsp.   fresh lemon zest
-             A few sprigs of mint (for garnish)

Instructions:
Combine condensed milk, evaporated milk, lemon zest, and fresh mint and stir. Combine berries and milk mixture together. Serve with a sprig of mint for garnish.

CHAPTER 9

Burgers and Blessings

SUGGESTED FOR MEMORIAL DAY

This is my commandment: love one another as I love you. No one has greater

love than this, to lay down one's life for one's friends.

JOHN 15: 12-13

There was a time in the not-too-distant past when families would take a picnic to the cemetery once or twice a year and spend the day caring for the family plot and reminiscing about relatives. In those cemeteries, many graves had a special tribute: a small United States flag signifying military service. Memorial Day has its roots in the custom of honoring the fallen with those flags on Decoration Day.

Flags are still put out each May in our national military cemeteries like Arlington, where there is a wreath-laying ceremony at the Tomb of the Unknowns. Flags are also displayed in communities where there are active veterans groups. But increasingly, Memorial Day is associated with a three-day weekend and the start of the summer vacation season. Families can make sure the meaning of the day is not lost to them or their neighbors by teaching the significance of Memorial Day as part of their celebration.

Taking the time to consider the cost of freedom and the bravery of those who are called to military service is not a political statement. In fact, the freedom to have opposing views and express them without fear is one of the values our military defends. Our military history is marked by battles fought to liberate people and protect them from tyranny, not to gain territory or impose our authority. Memorial Day honors those who were willing to leave behind their comforts so that others might be helped. Their goal was peace, not punishment. They were not anxious to die, but they acknowledged that risk when they took on the responsibility. Our heroes are born not of conquest but of compassion.

Because of the terrible things they witnessed, many of our living military heroes have been reluctant to talk about their war experiences. It has taken the work of interviewers like Tom Brokaw to give us a true picture of those who served in World War II. Journalists have extensively covered more recent wars, and the bravery of those who have risked or even sacrificed their lives to protect others is now widely documented. The more we know, the more we understand why it is right to preserve the true purpose of Memorial Day and make sure our children understand the human cost of the freedoms they know.

> *Memorial Day honors those who were willing to leave behind their comforts so that others might be helped.*

Your observance need not feel like a funeral—far from it. This is a time to savor what has been secured for you, including the fun of filling the backyard with family and friends to enjoy the first barbecue of the season. But start the day with a prayer and by hanging your United States flag from your porch or flagpole and placing smaller flags on your table. Do a little pre-gathering research on local Medal of Honor winners or military heroes. Find out about military veterans in your own family.

You may be surprised to discover that the reason an elderly aunt never married was not because she was never asked, but because her fiancé was a casualty in the Normandy invasion or was aboard a ship that was hit by enemy fire. Your own family history may provide reasons to make Memorial Day a more personal holiday celebrated not just with burgers but also with a prayer.

Your own family history may provide reasons to make Memorial Day a more personal day.

Let's Talk

Which freedoms do you most appreciate?

What do you consider worth defending, even worth dying for?

Do you have family or friends in the military right now?

Would you consider military service as an option for yourself?

We currently have an all-volunteer military.

What are the pros and cons of that policy?

In some parts of the world, teens are willing to become suicide bombers, and their parents take pride in that.

How would you attempt to change the mind of someone who had decided to become a suicide bomber?

The members of some religious groups are pacifists; Quakers and Mennonites are two examples.

How did the members of those groups fulfill their military obligation when they were drafted?

Was that appropriate or a violation of their convictions?

Let's Listen

Numbers 10:9   1 Chronicles 12   Psalm 106:3   2 Timothy 2

Let's Cook

FOUR BURGER IDEAS

This menu transforms the humble hamburger into a gourmet dish and your backyard into the neighborhood's favorite bistro. But before you sit down to eat, take a few moments to express your gratitude for those who have served our country and to pray for the protection of all those who serve today.

> *Make the chef's work as easy as possible by preparing ingredients in advance and using baskets or trays to get everything out to the grill area in as few trips as possible.*

Burgers with Four Separate Toppings

Serves: 4 | Prep Time: 15 Minutes | Cooking Time: 10 Minutes

Basic Hamburger Meat (Preparation)

Ingredients:

1 lb.	ground beef
1 tsp.	salt and pepper
1 packet	onion soup mix (or 1 medium onion, finely chopped with 1 tsp. garlic powder)

Instructions:

Combine all of the ingredients using your hands to incorporate all of the flavors. Divide the ground beef into 4 burger patties and follow the instructions for each burger!

Burger #1: Bleu Cheese and Barbecue Sauce

Ingredients:

2 Tbs.	bleu cheese (or Monterey Jack)
2 Tbs.	barbecue sauce

Instructions:

Combine the barbecue sauce with the crumbled bleu cheese in a bowl and mix. Use 1/2 of this combination and mix with one of the hamburger patties. Reshape the meat into a hamburger patty and cook on a grill for about 4-5 minutes on each side. When burger is cooked, top with the remaining mixture for a messy but tasty treat!

[Recipe continues on next page]

Burgers with Four Separate Toppings (continued)
Burger #2: Sweet Ginger Soy

Ingredients:

2 tsp.	sugar
2 Tbs.	soy sauce
1 tsp.	fresh lemon juice
¼ tsp.	fresh ginger, minced

Instructions:

Combine all the ingredients and heat in a pan over medium heat until flavors are fully incorporated. Use ½ of this combination and mix with one of the hamburger patties. Reshape the meat into a hamburger patty and cook on a grill for about 4-5 minutes on each side. When burger is cooked, top with the remaining mixture, or brush onto the bun for extra flavor!

Burger #3: Pizza Burger

Ingredients:

4 Tbs.	tomato sauce
¼ tsp.	garlic powder
½	onion, chopped
2 Tbs.	butter
¼ tsp.	salt
3 pinches	black pepper
2-4	pepperoni slices, finely chopped
2 Tbs.	mozzarella cheese, grated

Instructions:

Melt butter in a saucepan and sauté onions and garlic together. Add tomato sauce and cook for about 3-4 minutes. Season with salt and pepper, stir and set aside. Use ½ of this combination and the pepperoni and mix with one of the hamburger patties. Reshape the meat into a hamburger patty and cook on a grill for about 4-5 minutes on each side. Pour the rest of the sauce over the hamburger and top with cheese. Let this cook until cheese is melted.

Burger #4: California Avocado Burger

Ingredients:

1	avocado
½	lime, juiced
3 Tbs.	sour cream
¼ tsp.	salt
1 pinch	garlic powder
2 pinches	black pepper
1 tsp.	fresh cilantro, chopped

Instructions:

Cut avocado in half and spoon out the fruit into a bowl. Add lime juice, salt, pepper, garlic powder, cilantro, and sour cream. Using a fork, mash all of the ingredients together until you have a guacamole-style mix. Top off cooked burger with 1½ teaspoons of the mixture. Use the rest as a dip for potato or tortilla chips!

CHAPTER 10
Just Like Dad
SUGGESTED FOR FATHER'S DAY

Fathers, do not provoke your children to anger,

but bring them up with the training and instruction of the Lord.

EPHESIANS 6: 4

Could there be a more important assignment than that of father? It is the relationship intended to give even the youngest child his or her first glimpse of what God Himself is like. The qualities of a loving father reflect those of our Heavenly Father. Human fathers guide and shape their children in ways that will assure them the spiritual quality of life God intends.

Regardless of their personal gifts, fathers are expected to be able to do an amazing array of tasks. They need to be able to assemble everything from swing sets and bunk beds, to half-pipes and doll houses. They have to fix anything they're presented and, if possible, make it look easy so their child has bragging rights when the playground conversation turns to who has the best dad. They should be able to look at math homework and explain how to do it better than the teacher did. And they should have a schedule that allows them plenty of time to coach Little League or be a Scout leader.

Dads also have the tough job of setting limits. This is so difficult to do well that the Apostle Paul reminds fathers not to be harsh as they make and enforce the rules. They are to look to the Father and place their emphasis on training and instruction that brings their children close to God. Even the most outwardly compliant child will be angered by a human father whose manner of discipline is alien to the ways of the Heavenly Father, and that anger may lead to great pain for the entire family.

A father who commits to modeling God before his family will want to know God well. He will be a man of prayer, seeking the wisdom, patience, and love that God exhibits toward His children.

The qualities of a loving father reflect those of our Heavenly Father.

He will not let his children give in to fear. Instead, he will be right there with them as they face down fears and conquer them. He will not indulge their selfish interest in their own comfort. He will teach them to see and care for the needy around them so that they might better appreciate all they receive from him. He will prepare his children for their own marriages by following the biblical instruction to love their mother like Christ loved the Church. He will give them a clear understanding of what really matters by arranging his schedule to show that faith and family are higher priorities than wealth and pleasure. In turn, his children will bless him for teaching them what God is like.

It is a sad reality that in our society many children are growing up in homes without a human father. But it is wrong to call them fatherless. God has given a special promise to these children and their mothers. He says that HE will be their Father, and HE will sustain them. They are not alone, and they are not unloved. One of the ways God fulfills His promise is by bringing godly men into their lives, men who are equipped to mentor, counsel, and encourage. These role models may be in a child's life for many years, or God may send them for a special task. No matter what their specific role, they bring with them blessings and tangible proof that God is true to His word. Father's Day is the perfect occasion to acknowledge fathers and fatherly figures and let them know how important their influence has been.

Even though Father's Day is not a religious holiday, you can show your father how much you consider him a gift to your family by giving him a special gift. As much as dads appreciate ties and shirts, what they really enjoy is time with the family when the emphasis is on fun. This is a day for all his favorites, maybe even a day at the ballpark. Whatever you plan, just make sure Dad knows he's the guest of honor!

As much as dads appreciate ties and shirts, what they really enjoy is family time with the emphasis on fun.

Let's Talk

Do you think it's harder to be a mom or a dad? Why?

What is your father's greatest strength? Why do you think so?

What is your father's least favorite activity?

Which television fathers are the most realistic?

What's your favorite memory of time spent with your dad?

*Do you have friends who have difficult relationships with their fathers?
How does that affect their relationship with God?*

How do you think Jesus might have celebrated Father's Day with Saint Joseph?

Let's Listen

Genesis 37   Exodus 20:12   Proverbs 17: 5-7   Luke 15

Let's Cook

RIB EYE STEAKS WITH SWEETENED BLEU CHEESE CILANTRO BUTTER, FRESH SPINACH IN WARM BACON DRESSING

Pull out the old recipes for those dishes like Mom used to make, or surprise Dad with a menu that's just for him. No dainty tea sandwiches here!

Chill the sweet bleu cheese cilantro butter in a fancy mold to create a decoration for the steaks!

Rib Eye Steaks

Serves: 4 | Prep Time: 60 Minutes (including marinade) | Cooking Time: 15 Minutes

Ingredients:

4	rib eye steaks
2 tsp.	green peppercorns (optional)
2 tsp.	salt
1 tsp.	black pepper
1 tsp.	garlic powder
4 tsp.	Worcestershire sauce
4 tsp.	olive oil
4 tsp.	fresh cilantro, finely chopped
½ C	crumbled bleu cheese
4 Tbs.	butter
2 tsp.	honey
1	lemon, cut into 4 wedges

Instructions:

Prepare grill or turn oven to broil. Season rib eyes with salt, pepper, garlic powder, olive oil, and Worcestershire sauce and marinate for about 1 hour.

Optional: Crush green peppercorns by putting in a plastic bag and pressing with a flat frying pan. Remove peppercorns from bag and distribute over the steaks, pressing the crushed peppercorns into the meat.

In a separate bowl, add the bleu cheese, cilantro, butter, and honey and mix together. If necessary, heat for 30 seconds in the microwave to help the melting and mixing process. Set aside in refrigerator until ready to serve.

To cook steaks, place rib eyes directly on the heat for 5-7 minutes on each side for medium rare steaks. After the steaks are cooked, scoop a teaspoon of the sweetened bleu cheese butter to melt over the hot steaks. Serve with a lemon wedge to add another level of fresh flavor.

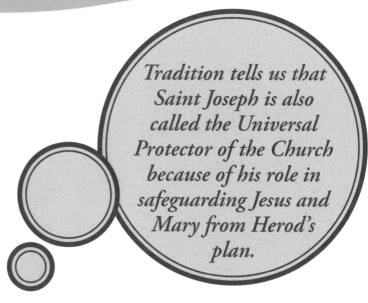

Tradition tells us that Saint Joseph is also called the Universal Protector of the Church because of his role in safeguarding Jesus and Mary from Herod's plan.

Fresh Spinach in Warm Bacon Dressing

Serves: 4 | Prep Time: 10 Minutes | Cooking Time: 5 Minutes

Ingredients:

8 C	fresh baby spinach leaves (2 bags pre-washed spinach)
8	strips thick cut bacon
3 tsp.	strawberry jam
3 tsp.	cider vinegar
3 tsp.	mustard
¼ tsp.	black pepper

Instructions:

Cut bacon into ¼ inch strips. Cook in a pan until crispy and place to the side. Remove pan from heat and drain half of the bacon grease. With the remaining bacon grease still in the pan, add strawberry jam, vinegar, mustard, and black pepper and stir together. Return pan to heat and add spinach. Toss everything in the pan until spinach begins to wilt. Remove from heat immediately and sprinkle with crumbled pieces of bacon. Serve warm.

CHAPTER 11
Be Mine

… that Christ may dwell in your hearts through faith; that you, rooted and grounded in love, may have strength to comprehend with all the holy ones what is the breadth and length and height and depth, and to know the love of Christ that surpasses knowledge.…

EPHESIANS 3: 17-19A

The Bible teaches that believers are new creations in Christ and that our regeneration extends all the way to our cores—to our hearts. What an awesome thought! Jesus' love for those who come to Him in faith is so complete that He offers His heart as a replacement for their cold and stony one. It's a total transplant, one that cuts away the blockages caused by old hurts and the disease of sin and unbelief. When we trust in Christ, He puts His heart in us so we can love like Him and learn to live like Him!

The enormity of this gift and its implications is so radical we are tempted to dismiss it as impossible. The enemy of our souls comes to accuse us and remind us of all our failures. When we give in to Satan's schemes instead of trusting God's promises, we revert to our old habits of relying on our flawed feelings and judgment. We remain pressed down by old guilt. Our lives are cold and empty unless we take the time to measure our version of love against God's.

Even if we work hard at trying to be kind, even if we think we are loving compared to other people, we can't get beyond caring on a human level. Human love gets tangled up in human concerns like reciprocity and worthiness.

The love that comes from God is entirely different from human love. The source of this love is uniquely divine rather than human and its outworking is unconditional, not dependent on any merit. Paul writes to the believers in Corinth, "Love is patient, love is kind. It is not jealous, it is not pompous, it is not inflated, it is not rude, it does not seek its own interests, it is not quick-tempered, it does not brood over injury, it does not rejoice over wrongdoing but rejoices with the truth. It bears all things, believes all things, hopes all things, endures all things. Love never fails."

> *"Agape" is the Greek word for God's love, which is a sacrificial type of love.*

When we love with Christ's love we are able to love without concern for ourselves. We are able to love without concern for our reputations or our reward because they are protected and provided by Christ. We love because we are loved. We forgive because Christ forgives us. We give because Christ gives to us. Our decision to act out of love is no longer dependent on our ability to love. Instead, we consider the greatness of Christ's love toward us and how He might be honored as His love is expressed through us as we serve others.

Consider the impact of shifting perspective like this. Motivated by Christ's love, we would be able to put aside the things that distress us or make us feel uncomfortable and focus our attention on the people who need our love, whether we find them in our streets and shelters, our prisons, our hospitals, or our own homes. Expecting no more than Christ did from the people He came to die for, we would remember Him and reflect His selfless love for us. Because of His love, we can love our enemies and do good to those who hate us. How many family disagreements would be resolved in an instant if one person in the dispute decided to let Christ love through him or her, speaking and acting out of kindness instead of anger? How many people would find emotional and spiritual healing if they were able to seek God's attitude toward a person who has done them a great wrong and choose forgiveness over revenge or hatred? How many relationships would be restored if we cared more about repair and restoration than we did about demanding our "right" to restitution? How many prodigal sons and daughters are longing for the welcoming hug of a parent who loves them and wants them to have a fresh start?

These are not theoretical questions. Nothing provides a clearer picture of our faith than our life of love. We may talk all we want about our virtues, but the truth is exposed in how brightly Christ's love shines through us.

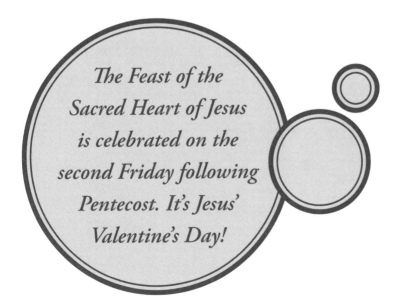

The Feast of the Sacred Heart of Jesus is celebrated on the second Friday following Pentecost. It's Jesus' Valentine's Day!

Let's Talk

How is God's love different from human love?

Who is difficult for you to love? What happens when the challenge changes from how you can love that person to how God can love that person through you?

Who is the most loving person you know? What qualities do they exhibit?

Sometimes teens are pressured on dates to "prove their love." Why is such a request proof that the person making it is not exhibiting love?

Jesus showed love to the outcasts of His time on earth.
In your community, who are considered the outcasts, and how might you show them God's love?

In the next twenty-four hours, what three things could you do to share God's love in your neighborhood?

Let's Listen

I Corinthians 13   Galatians 4: 6   Colossians 3: 15-17

I Thessalonians 3: 11-13   I Peter 3: 15

Let's Cook

Who would Jesus feed today? This is an opportunity to exhibit love by preparing a meal for someone who would not expect it or for someone who is a stranger in your community, like an international student. Perhaps you and your family could be a part of preparing and serving a meal for many by volunteering at a community shelter, your local "Meals on Wheels," or a similar community outreach program. This menu offers a special meal – from the heart!

Osso Bucco (Braised Veal Shank)

Serves: 4 | Prep Time: 25 Minutes | Cooking Time: 2 Hours

Ingredients:

4	veal shanks
2 tsp.	salt
1 tsp.	black pepper
½ C	flour
4 Tbs.	olive oil
2 cloves	garlic, minced
1	small onion, finely minced
2 stalks	celery, chopped ¼ inch
2	carrots, chopped ¼ inch
2 C	dry white wine
1 C	beef broth
4 Tbs.	tomato paste
2	bay leaves

Instructions:

Preheat oven to 275 degrees. When preparing the shanks, leave the bone in the center. Season the shanks with salt and pepper and dredge in flour. Shake off extra flour. Add olive oil to a hot pan and carefully sear the shanks, cooking 2-4 minutes on each side or until a brown caramelized color. Remove shanks and place in a deep baking dish, setting aside to prepare the vegetables and braising liquids.

To the hot pan, add chopped garlic, onion, celery, and carrots. Let cook in the oil for 2-3 minutes. Add 2 cups of dry white wine, beef broth, and tomato paste. Use whisk to mix drippings from the bottom of the pan. Add bay leaves and let simmer for 2-3 minutes, allowing alcohol to cook out. Add 2-3 pinches of salt and pepper to taste.

Pour the wine and broth mixture over the shanks and cover with foil. Use a fork to poke some holes in the foil to allow steam to be released. Cook in the oven for 1½ -2 hours.

Garlic Whipped Mashed Potatoes

Serves: 4 | Prep Time: 10 Minutes | Cooking Time: 25 Minutes

Ingredients:

1 qt.	water
4	large potatoes
2 tsp.	salt
½ tsp.	pepper
4 Tbs.	butter
2 cloves	garlic, minced
½ C	heavy whipping cream
3-4 tsp.	fresh parsley, minced

Instructions:

Boil water in a large pot. Peel and cut potatoes in quarters and add to boiling water. Cook for approximately 20-25 minutes or until potatoes are fork-tender. Ladle out 1 cup of starchy water and save. Drain the rest of the water and keep potatoes in pot. Using a potato masher, begin to mash the potatoes.

In a separate microwave-safe bowl, melt butter, garlic, heavy whipping cream, salt, pepper, and parsley together and cook for about 1 minute. Add this garlic butter to the potatoes and continue to mash or whip with a hand blender. Add saved starchy potato water as needed for desired consistency.

When you show love by feeding the hungry, you offer far more than just a meal.

CHAPTER 12
Living in Liberty
SUGGESTED FOR INDEPENDENCE DAY

For you were called for freedom, brothers. But do not use this freedom as an opportunity for the flesh; rather, serve one another through love. For the whole law is fulfilled in one statement, namely, "You shall love your neighbor as yourself."

GALATIANS 5: 13-14

As the Constitutional Congress closed its deliberations in 1787, one of the anxious observers outside the hall asked Benjamin Franklin, "Well Doctor, what have we got— a monarchy or a republic?" Franklin replied, "A republic, if you can keep it." Our founders, especially the wise elder statesmen like Franklin, knew the government they were establishing for the United States of America was an experiment. Its success depended more on the commitment of its citizens than the skill of its designers. If the citizens could trust the leaders they chose and hold them to a standard of excellence as they performed their duties, the experiment would be a model for the rest of the world. If the citizens abdicated their responsibilities and ceded all the authority to those in power, the experiment would be a failure.

While our record is not perfect, our experimental republic is well into its third century. Our form of government has been replicated in other nations that have gained their freedom. And it remains the model for those who believe that the biblical principle of servant leadership is the ideal for those who govern.

This principle is so important to us it has been imbedded in our American idioms. The term we use for government work in the United States is "public service." That term denotes our expectation that those who obtain elective office or accept appointments in our government take up their positions with the intent to uphold the law and serve others fairly and honorably, even when that service comes at a personal cost to them. We will not tolerate unethical behavior in any official, even if that conduct can be defended as meeting the letter of the law.

The biblical principle of servant leadership should be the ideal for those who govern.

Citizens uphold their end of the contract by following the law, being informed about issues and candidates, and casting their votes for those whom they believe most capable and most fit for the responsibility of office. Citizens also bear a responsibility to make sure the promises made in a political campaign are actually kept. This is not easy work, but it is not impossible. A call or an e-mail is all it takes to make your opinion heard. The people who are most effective in office are those who want to know what their constituents think about the decisions they're making in committees and open sessions.

Parents often tell their children that only in America can any child grow up to be president. That's a tradition we can protect by encouraging any child with an interest in government to pursue that high goal. But America also needs service-minded people who will take some time from their full-time careers to be school board members, county commissioners, mayors, and town council representatives. If the official biographies on the United States Senate and

> *Let's remember that freedom is a gift that should never be abused. Freedom is not cheap!*

House of Representatives websites are a good indicator, these local offices can also be great places from which to launch a career in Congress, or even in the White House.

One of the luxuries of liberty is the freedom to be critical. In this country, late-night comedians fill their monologues with jokes about the people in power. The most successful politicians learn to take the jabs with a smile. One famous United States senator collected thirty years worth of political cartoons that took aim at him and covered the walls of his office with the best of them. Every year, the president is the guest of honor at dinners hosted by the National Press Club and the White House Correspondents, getting his share of laughs by turning the tables on the people who make their living finding fault with him. This give-and-take is an American tradition that exemplifies the strength of our democracy.

All of our American freedoms—the right to vote, the right to worship openly, an independent press—are genuine blessings. We pass them from one generation to the next by taking care to assure the strength of our democracy and by showing our children that we value the privilege of liberty. Many of our parents and grandparents crossed oceans, often risking their lives, so their children could have better lives in America. When we celebrate our country, we honor our founders and our families for the heritage they gave us: life in the land of the free and the home of the brave.

Let's Talk

Which American freedom would you most hate to lose? Why?

Which freedom would you be willing to give up in exchange for something else?

Have you ever read the words to the national anthem? Do you know its background story?

If you were asked to nominate a different song to be our national anthem, what would you pick? Why?

Do you know someone who came to America to escape political tyranny?
Have you ever asked about his or her experiences?

What is your favorite Fourth of July family tradition?
What is a tradition you'd like to add to your celebration?

Have you ever attended a government session or meeting?
Have you ever thought about running for office? Which one?

Let's Listen

Psalm 119: 44-46   Isaiah 61   Luke 4: 14-21   Galatians 5

Let's Cook

ITALIAN SAUSAGES WITH ORANGES, CILANTRO, BLEU CHEESE AND BARBECUE SAUCE, RAMEN SALAD WITH GRILLED CORN AND SCALLIONS

Freedom is not just about government, it's also personal. This is a good day to encourage those who are trying to free themselves from bad habits that have taken away their freedom. Expand your guest list to include someone who will appreciate your hospitality and your support.

This easy-to-make recipe isn't always so easy to eat. But as with Sloppy Joes, the messiness is worth it!

Italian Sausages
Serves: 6 | Prep Time: 15 Minutes | Cooking Time: 40 Minutes

Ingredients:

12	sausages
3 tsp.	olive oil
1 tsp.	orange zest
1	orange, juiced (approximately 2-3 tablespoons)
¼ tsp.	red pepper flakes
¼ tsp.	salt
¼ tsp.	pepper
½ C	bleu cheese (cheddar cheese may be substituted)
½ C	barbecue sauce
12	hotdog buns

Instructions:

Preheat oven to 375 degrees. Prepare sausages by cutting a 1/4 inch slit longways to create a "pocket" to stuff. Place sausages on a baking pan, allowing at least 1/2 inch separation.

In a separate bowl, mix the orange juice, orange zest, olive oil, bleu/cheddar cheese, red pepper flakes, and barbecue sauce. Mix thoroughly. Using a teaspoon, insert some of the barbecue and cheese mix into the sausages. Bake sausages for 35-40 minutes and serve on hotdog buns for easy eating.

Ramen Salad with Grilled Corn

Serves: 6 | Prep Time: 25 Minutes | Cooking Time: 10 Minutes

Ingredients:

2 packs	ramen noodles (do not use the spice packet)
8 C	shredded iceberg lettuce
2	ears corn on the cob
2	scallion stems, minced
2	carrots, shredded
4 tsp.	soy sauce
4 Tbs.	olive oil
4 Tbs.	white or apple cider vinegar
½ tsp.	salt
¼ tsp.	pepper

Instructions:

Fire up grill to high heat. Clean and prepare corn by pulling back the husk, but leave it on the cob. Remove the corn silk and discard. After the corn is cleaned, return the leaves to cover the cob and soak the whole corn on the cob in water for about 10 minutes. Place the whole corn on the grill for approximately 10-15 minutes, turning every 2-3 minutes. The water from the soaking will steam the corn, while the grilled leaves will add a smoky flavor to it. Once cooked, let corn cool before shaving off the kernels into a bowl.

Prepare rest of salad by breaking up the ramen noodles in bowl. Add all of the other ingredients and mix well so that the noodles begin to soak up the liquids. Let the salad sit in the liquids for at least 10 minutes before adding salt and pepper to taste.

America, America, God shed His grace on thee!

CHAPTER 13
Generation to Generation
SUGGESTED FOR GRANDPARENT'S DAY

Great is the LORD and worthy of high praise; God's grandeur is beyond understanding.

One generation praises your deeds to the next and proclaims your mighty works.

They speak of the splendor of your majestic glory, tell of your wonderful deeds.

PSALM 145:3-5

In our society, grandparents often occupy a very different position than they do in other parts of the world, and that is a great loss. Instead of being our close neighbors, grandparents can live thousands of miles away. Leisurely, daily contact has given way to weekly phone calls and event-packed visits during which most of the time is taken up in the exchange of highlights and data. The end result can be families who know a lot of facts about each other, but do not actually know each other.

Grandparents are supposed to play an important role in the lives of their grandchildren, but not the one often seen. It is not the grandparents' place to impose their opinions on family management or child discipline. Nor is it their right to exert influence or use bribes to convince their grandchildren to follow their directives when the decision should be the parents'. Grandparents are called to a much higher responsibility.

It is the privilege of grandparents to offer perspective. They have not earned their experience so they can be managers, but so they can be encouragers. When parents are unsure they can manage the task of parenthood, grandparents aren't there to argue or to rescue, but to provide a gentle reminder that along with the gift of children, God provides everything parents need to care for that child.

All those years in the stands as number one soccer mom or team dad are actually training for the big leagues when our sons and daughters become parents themselves and need reassurance that they are doing a great job. The same rules supportive moms and dads follow with their children after every ball game apply when supporting a parent. Focus on the positive. Remind rookie parents of the things they are doing well as they learn to care for their own children. In the grand scheme of things, it makes no difference at all if grandchildren have a different sleep and meal schedule than the one that worked for their parents. Grandparents are doing their job when they ignore all those incidentals and concentrate on the sweet sound of young parents reading a classic fairy tale or praying with their little one at bedtime. Grandparents are supposed to watch from the stands and tell the new team what looks good, cheering hard, especially on the tough days.

Grandparents also have the matchless responsibility of freely loving grandchildren without being distracted by jelly smears, unmade beds, or grades. Without subverting the rules parents have established, grandparents can provide the hugs and winks that tell children they are doing okay even when they color outside the

It is the privilege of grandparents to offer perspective.

lines. Spilled milk, a broken dish, a ball through the neighbor's window, a dented fender, or a missed curfew won't upset a grandparent with a good memory. That means everything to a child surrounded by frowns and the prospect of being grounded. Building a record of reliable acceptance creates channels of communication that will stay strong in the rockiest of times, including times of teen rebellion against parental authority.

Above every other responsibility and privilege that might come to grandparents is the one laid out again and again in the Bible—faith formation. Grandparents are entrusted with recounting God's goodness. They must tell the stories of grace over and over so their children and grandchildren can memorize the details and be ready to pass this history to the next generation. Grandparents know how God worked in the years before they were born, and they know their stories that must be added to the family history. Their testimony of faith and encouragement makes an impression that remains long after they are no longer alive.

Finally, and most importantly, grandparents have the responsibility to pray for their grandchildren.

Grandparents can provide the hugs and winks that tell children they are doing okay.

The work of prayer is not hindered by distance or age or even infirmity. Can there be any more treasured inheritance than the knowledge that a loving grandparent never stopped praying, never stopped believing, never stopped trusting in God's faithfulness to all generations?

Let's Talk

Do you think older people are stereotyped in our society?

Why do some kids find it easier to talk to their grandparents than to their parents?

Do you have a favorite memory or story about each of your grandparents?

What plans for life did your grandparents have at your age?
What dreams for the future do they have now?

If you could give each of your grandparents one special day,
and there were no limits on your plans, what would you do?

What do you think of as old? What are the signs of old age?

How often should grandchildren be in touch with their own grandparents?

Let's Listen

Genesis 9   Joshua 22   Psalm 33

Psalm 105   Luke 1: 46-56

Let's Cook

MAHIMAHI WITH CAPER MUSTARD SAUCE
ORZO PASTA WITH BUTTER AND PEAS

If your grandparents are nearby, throw them a party with heart-healthy versions of their favorite foods or surprise them with new dishes picked out just for them. If your grandparents are far away, surprise them with a delivery of foods they'll enjoy, along with the latest family pictures. If they are no longer alive, use Grandparent's Day as an opportunity to honor their memory by visiting lonely seniors who are in full-time care facilities.

> *My grandparents love seafood! This recipe offers a taste that's different from the way they would have had it in the Philippines.*

Mahimahi

Serves: 6 | Prep Time: 10 Minutes | Cooking Time: 15 Minutes

Ingredients:

6	mahimahi fillets
1½ C	seasoned breadcrumbs
2	eggs, beaten with 2 teaspoons water
3 Tbs.	olive oil
3 tsp.	butter
1½ tsp.	mustard
3 tsp.	capers with juice
½ tsp.	salt
¼ tsp.	pepper
1	lemon, juiced
2 Tbs.	parsley, chopped (for garnish and flavor)

Instructions:

Season mahimahi with salt and pepper. Dredge fillets in breadcrumbs. Dip fillets in egg mixture, and then dredge in breadcrumbs again.

Heat olive oil in pan, and carefully place fillets in hot oil. Cook 3-5 minutes on each side. Once cooked, remove and place on a serving plate. To the same pan, add butter, mustard, lemon juice, and capers. Salt and pepper to taste. Let the butter melt, and let the flavors cook together. Pour the sauce over the breaded mahimahi. Sprinkle the parsley over the fish for garnish and extra flavor.

Orzo Pasta with Butter and Peas

Serves: 6 | Prep Time: 15 Minutes | Cooking Time: 5 Minutes

Ingredients:

1 ½ C	orzo pasta
1 ½ C	frozen peas
½ tsp.	salt
¼ tsp.	pepper
¼ tsp.	garlic powder
3 Tbs.	butter
½ C	Parmesan cheese, grated

Instructions:

Boil orzo pasta in water. When pasta is almost cooked, add frozen peas to the boiling water. When pasta is cooked and peas are soft, drain the water leaving only a few tablespoons of water in the pot. Add butter, salt, pepper, and garlic powder, and mix well to incorporate flavors. Add fresh grated Parmesan cheese, and mix together before serving.

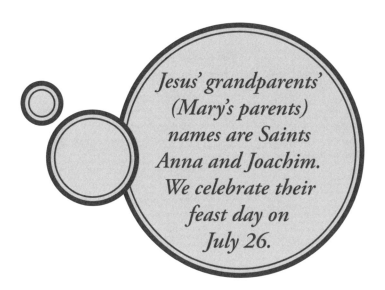

Jesus' grandparents' (Mary's parents) names are Saints Anna and Joachim. We celebrate their feast day on July 26.

CHAPTER 14
Only a Game
WINNING AND LOSING

(But) whatever gains I had, these I have come to consider a loss because of Christ.

More than that, I even consider everything as a loss because of the supreme good of

knowing Christ Jesus my Lord. For his sake I have accepted the loss of all things

and I consider them so much rubbish, that I may gain Christ.

PHILIPPIANS 3:7-8

Competition is a basic component of human interaction. It is a God-given gift that teaches perseverance, leadership, cooperation, graciousness, and humility.

We usually think of competition in connection with sports, but competition is a part of our family relationships and our friendships. We see it when we vie for good parking spaces and the best position at the grocery checkout, and it certainly shows up in the classroom and the office.

Our country is fueled by competition; it is an essential component of our free enterprise system—the element that pushes businesses to "try harder." Successful companies and professionals want to offer better products, service, and prices so they will be known as the best in their field. Both consumers and businesses benefit in this environment. The consumer gains from being served by someone who is always trying to improve, and the business profits from increased traffic.

Competition is the power behind invention and exploration, too. Scientists from different nations have raced to find cures for diseases, recover and convert raw materials into valuable resources, and study outer space and the depths of the ocean. Millions have benefited from these efforts.

Millions more have enjoyed the excitement and pride of supporting their favorite teams, from Little League to the pros. The United States is a late entry in soccer's World Cup series, but we try to make up for that with our efforts to win gold at the Olympics. Americans often measure Olympic success by comparing the number of medals we've won to those won by the Germans or the Russians. But we can lose sight of the real value of the games when we do that. The winners are not just the athletes who finished first, second, and third, but those who participated and did their best, no matter where they finished in the standings.

That is the philosophy of competition we need to affirm in our families. Doing your best and playing by the rules are the true marks of success in any contest. Wins and losses are just statistics. Competition is not something to avoid; it's something to embrace because it motivates us to action. We cannot and should not insulate our kids or ourselves from the risks of the arena. Instead, we have to train for genuine success.

> *True competition brings out the best, not the worst, in people.*

In the classic poem "If," Kipling offers a prescription for true success in life. He says that knowing how to handle both winning and losing is one of the keys to having all that life has to offer.

His admonition is to "treat those two imposters just the same." In other words, we should not become conceited in victory or despairing in loss. But how do we find that balance, and more importantly, how do we build it into the lives of young people?

It is a daily process of celebrating the success of good efforts, the strengths that make each person special, and the love that is guaranteed in your family. This steady build up of the positive and the permanent provides a cushion that puts both winning and losing into context.

The hurt of a loss like missing a play on the field, not being picked for a squad, finishing second in a class election, or breaking up with a boyfriend or girlfriend takes its rightful place as an event, not a defining moment. In the minutes and days after any loss, the best messages are hugs and the acknowledgement of pain. In this "teachable moment," the most important lesson your child needs is that you are standing by to help and to encourage. There is time enough for secondary lessons that will help turn the next competition into a win.

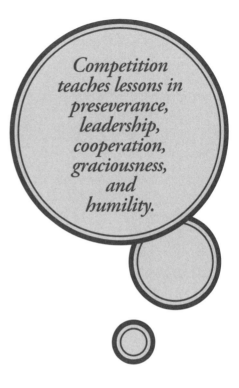

Competition teaches lessons in preseverance, leadership, cooperation, graciousness, and humility.

Understanding real success and knowing the hurt of loss are essential to learning how to win graciously. There is nothing less attractive than gloating in victory. Winners who acknowledge the hard work of their opponent, the efforts of those who helped put them in a position to win, and the divine Providence that allowed them victory display the qualities of people worthy to be known as champions.

Let's Talk

Who do you compete with at home and at school? What do you compete over?

Who is your favorite athlete? How does he or she respond to winning and losing?

Some schools have eliminated team tryouts and let anyone who is interested join the team of his or her choice. Do you think this is a good idea? Why or why not?

How do you feel when you hear someone's parent yelling at him or her from the stands or after a game? Why do some parents behave like that?

Is losing related to being a loser?

If you were preparing an acceptance speech for an award, what would you say?

Let's Listen

Psalm 44   Proverbs 3   Isaiah 5: 8-30

Luke 9   Thessalonians 4: 9-12

Let's Cook

HEARTY BOLOGNESE AND GARLIC BREAD

Get your team together to celebrate good effort and lessons learned, no matter what the rankings look like. Reminisce about the fun moments and honor the unique contributions made by each team member. This is a good time to try out a casserole or pasta recipe. Serve it with a salad and let the team pitch in with their favorite appetizers and desserts.

Hearty Bolognese

Serves: 4 | Prep Time: 20 Minutes | Cooking Time: 20 Minutes

Ingredients:

1 box	thick spaghetti
¼ lb.	ground beef
¼ lb.	ground pork
¼ lb.	ground veal
½ C	onions, chopped
½ C	celery, chopped
¼ C	carrots, chopped
2	cloves garlic, chopped
½ C	heavy whipping cream
¼ C	fresh Parmesan cheese, grated
6 oz.	tomato paste
2	bay leaves
	(if dried, chop or grind in a pestle or food processor)
½ tsp.	salt
½ tsp.	pepper
½ C	mushrooms, sliced (optional)
3 Tbs.	olive oil
2 C	white wine
2-4 C	boiled pasta water
	(add according to the desired thickness of sauce)

Instructions:

Heat a large pot with olive oil. Sauté onions, celery, carrots, garlic, and bay leaves. Add the meat, salt, and pepper and cook thoroughly, mixing all of the ingredients together. Cook uncovered for about 10-15 minutes.

After meat is cooked, add wine and cream. Cook until alcohol smell dissipates, about 5 minutes. Add the tomato paste and mix thoroughly, creating a paste-like sauce.

Heat water to a boil and add pasta. When the pasta is cooked al dente, remove it from the water and place it into the sauce. Reserve 4-5 cups starchy water and gradually add into the sauce until it has a thick, chili-like consistency. Mix in Parmesan cheese to help thicken and flavor the sauce.

Mix pasta and sauce together. Top off each serving with a little more freshly grated Parmesan cheese and a drizzle of extra virgin olive oil.

Garlic Bread

Serves: 4 | Prep Time: 10 Minutes | Cooking Time: 10 Minutes

Ingredients:

2	mini baguettes
¼ C	mayonnaise
¼ tsp.	garlic powder
¼ tsp.	salt
¼ tsp.	black pepper
½ tsp.	parsley, freshly chopped

Instructions:

Preheat oven to 400 degrees. Cut mini baguettes in half, creating 4 equal sized open-faced buns.

In a bowl, mix mayonnaise, garlic powder, salt, pepper, and parsley. Using a spatula, evenly spread a coating of the mixture over each piece of bread.

Put the bread on a cookie sheet, and place in oven for 8-10 minutes or until the mayonnaise becomes golden brown.

(l-to-r)
Me; my father, Carlos Sr.;
and my brother, Carlos Jr.
in the early 1990s.

As a young man, I enjoyed competing in a martial art called Arnis, which is Philippine full-contact stick fighting. In 1991, I won a gold medal in my sparring division.

CHAPTER 15
You're Hired
LANDING A FIRST JOB

Then David said to his son Solomon: "Be firm and steadfast; go to work without fear or discouragement, for the LORD God, my God, is with you. He will not fail you or abandon you before you have completed all the work for the service of the house of the LORD."

1 CHRONICLES 28:20

It's a day parents think they long for—that day when the child who has depended on them for just about everything discovers the power of an income of his or her own.

The amount of that income doesn't matter. The significance is in the step toward independence and adulthood. It is indeed an event worth celebrating. Your child getting hired means an impartial judge has determined that he or she has valuable qualities that are in demand. Those qualities are most likely dependability, punctuality, and trustworthiness—qualities you have worked hard to instill, so it is a double cause for celebration.

Being the parent of an employee is different than being the parent of a student or a team member or a scout. There is no "parents' night" to attend, and no parent conferences where a child's boss gives a progress report, or a parent explains that an undone assignment was the result of an unexpected family outing. Aside from being alert to a situation that might be dangerous or illegal, parents have no standing with employers. They are not advocates for their child, and they are not participants in the relationship between employer and employee or employee and coworker or employee and customer.

This is not an easy transition to make. Parents are fiercely loyal. They do not like to hear that someone was displeased with their child. They want to step in when it seems their child is being treated unfairly. They worry about risks. They want to be first on their child's list of priorities. The feelings are reminiscent of the ones they had that day long ago, when it was time to walk out of the kindergarten classroom and let somebody else become a major influence in that child's life.

The support and encouragement you offer your new wage earner today will lay the groundwork for the two of you to talk in the future about one of the most important areas of your child's adult life. You are also helping to shape a pattern that will persist when that child is building a career. You and your child are entering a new phase of your relationship, and your ability to listen, to offer counsel when needed, and to encourage independence are more critical than ever.

When your child tells you the boss was grouchy or the customer was rude or the work was hard, you have to say, "I'm sorry to hear that. Do you want to talk about it?" You cannot say, "How dare he!" or "I hope you told her off!" or "You don't have to do that kind of job!"

Your goal is to let your child do the work of maturing—of figuring out how to deal with grouchy bosses and rude customers and the unpleasant parts of jobs. Why? Because experience in dealing with these realities is infinitely more instructive than hearing about them from you or the world's most gifted management consultant. Cranky Mr. Smith, who is never quite satisfied with

> *Be there to listen and to remind your new wage earner of his or her ability to meet any challenge.*

how his lawn gets cut, is good training for cranky Dr. Smith, who rarely has a positive word for the interns he supervises. Rude customers at the drive-in window are miniature versions of rude customers with impossible demands for delivery. Knowing how to be civil in the face of incivility cannot be learned in the abstract. Handling the necessary cleanups that come along with an evening of babysitting fosters the determination and confidence to confront the more difficult aspects in every job, even the ones that seem more glamorous.

Be there to listen and to remind your child of his or her ability to meet any challenge. Express your unconditional love and your pride. Try not to act surprised when the child who was happy to spend your income on life's extras is suddenly a little more frugal with his or her income. It may be hard to imagine, but the time is not far off when you will get an invitation to dinner with your child, and you will not be allowed to pick up the tab. That, too, will be a day for celebration!

As your child enters this new phase of maturity, your support and encouragement is more critical than ever.

Let's Talk

Why do you think it's hard for some kids to find their first jobs?

What are some ways to get over those hurdles?

What kinds of first jobs were available to your parents but aren't around anymore?
Why did they disappear? What kinds of part-time jobs are new to your generation?
Why were they created?

If you were to create a business, what would it be? How would you find customers?
What would you charge?

How would you respond to someone's criticism if you didn't think it was justified?

Do you think it's good for kids to have jobs of their own?
What are some valid reasons for kids not to work outside the home?

What would you buy with your own money? What would you save for?
What good cause would you give to?

Let's Listen

Genesis 2   Exodus 35   Matthew 20

John 6:25-59   I Thessalonians 4:11

Let's Cook

As we grow up, so should our tastes! Make this meal memorable by including something as new as the new job.

> *Tuna can be as simple as a sandwich or as fancy as sushi-grade Ahi!*

Seared Ahi Tuna Steaks

Serves: 4 | Prep Time: 15 Minutes | Cooking Time: 20 Minutes

Ingredients:

4	tuna steaks at least 1½ in. thick
½ C	Italian seasoned breadcrumbs
¼ tsp.	salt
¼ tsp.	pepper
2 Tbs.	olive oil
¼ C	mayonnaise
¼ tsp.	dried wasabi mix (or 1 tsp. of fresh-grated horseradish)
2	pinches paprika
1 Tbs.	fresh lemon juice

Instructions:

Season ahi tuna steaks with olive oil, salt, and pepper, then dredge in breadcrumbs.

Heat a nonstick pan over high heat. Right before putting the tuna on the pan, turn down flame to medium heat in order to sear but not burn the steaks. Cook for 2-3 minutes on each side for a rare tuna that will have a soft red color in the middle. To make the tuna well-done, cook each steak 5-7 minutes on each side.

To make the wasabi mayo, add the mayonnaise, wasabi mix or freshly grated horseradish, two pinches of paprika, and lemon juice into a bowl. Mix together.

Add a small dollop of the mayo to the top of each tuna steak as it is taken off the grill and ready to be served.

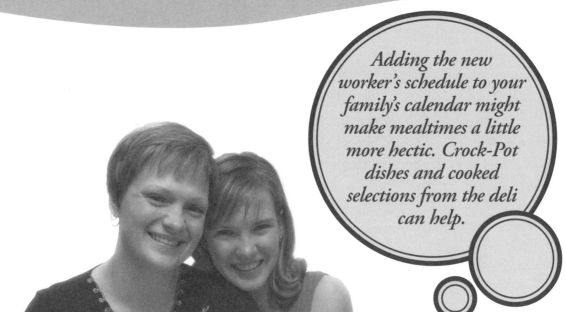

Adding the new worker's schedule to your family's calendar might make mealtimes a little more hectic. Crock-Pot dishes and cooked selections from the deli can help.

Pan Seared Eggplants

Serves: 4 | Prep Time: 10 Minutes | Cooking Time: 20 Minutes

Ingredients:

½	large eggplant, cut into ½ inch cubes (approx. 4-6 cups cubed eggplant)
¼ C	olive oil
1 clove	garlic, finely minced
2 tsp.	butter
6 Tbs.	soy sauce
6 tsp.	water
2 Tbs.	fresh lemon juice
½ tsp.	salt
½ tsp.	red pepper flakes
1 Tbs.	fresh parsley, minced

Instructions:

Heat olive oil in a large frying pan, and add garlic over high heat. Drop heat to medium, and add the eggplant. Let eggplant cook for approximately 12-15 minutes to soak up and fry in the hot oil. Occasionally stir the eggplant around so that you eventually see a seared brown color develop on its different sides. After eggplant becomes less firm, add butter, soy sauce, lemon juice, water, salt, and red pepper flakes. Mix together, and let simmer for about 5 minutes more. Prior to serving, sprinkle with the fresh, minced parsley.

CHAPTER 16
Hurts and Healing
RELATIONSHIPS

God is our refuge and our strength, an ever-present help in distress. Thus we do not

fear, though earth be shaken and mountains quake to the depths of the sea.

PSALM 46: 2-3

We all remember our child's first steps, first solo bike ride, first time on stage, first soccer match. Those successes are great highlights, but parents are better prepared for the rough teen years if they remember how they handled all the bumps, bruises, tears, and failures on the way to those picture-perfect moments. Parents will again need to put those coping skills to use as their teens master the skills of adulthood.

Just as the toddler stage helps a child get acquainted with physical capabilities like running, climbing, jumping, tumbling, and even dancing, the teen stage is when a child learns about emotions. The tears and tantrums and then total happiness kids experience in the early years will seem like scale models of the highs and lows you'll see in the years between the tenth or twelfth birthday and the nineteenth.

In the teen years, parents discover that there are no training wheels, knee-pads, or helmets they can supply their children to protect them from emotional bruising. They are no longer supervisors. They must learn to be trusted counselors. Veterans of this transition will be quick to say that it is more difficult than they could have imagined. Parents of teens must learn to listen carefully, speak wisely, know when to be silent, and love unconditionally.

The bumps and bruises of the teen years come from friendships, dating relationships, rejections, self-criticism, out-of-bounds behavior, and sometimes the misdeeds of adults who have abused a teen's trust. Parents can provide "first aid" by being available and approachable.

When a child says, "Do you have a minute?" you must be willing to put aside your tasks and offer your full attention. No matter how the ensuing conversation makes you feel, you have to be willing to hear the whole story without injecting your commentary. When it is your turn to speak, you must take your time and choose your words wisely. They will be salt or salve.

Begin with a restatement of your love for your child, your confidence in his or her value, and your certainty that God can bring good out of the worst of situations, even this one. Ask gentle questions about how he or she is feeling. Ask if there is anything you can do, unless the situation is potentially dangerous, in which case you must immediately take charge. Reaffirm your love and support as he or she works through the problem. If you sense that a hug would be welcomed at this moment, offer one.

> *A great way to deal with a broken heart is to humbly ask, "What can I learn from this pain?" It still hurts, but the pain has meaning and purpose for our future.*

As hard as it will be, resist any remark that your teen might read as belittlement. Do not say things like, "That's not so bad!" or "Plenty of fish in the sea," or "What did you do to cause this?" or "I should have known you couldn't handle that." Even that last remark, which sounds like self-criticism, is really a criticism of your child, just as each of the others attack his or her decision-making ability and behavior. The time for analysis might come, but this is not that time.

Instead, ask, "What would you like to do now?" and accommodate anything reasonable. Set a time when you will talk some more, and let your child have some space to think and refocus.

Use the time before that next conversation to pray for wisdom; have confidence that God will provide what you need. With the emotional thermostat turned down, you and your teen can look calmly at the source of the hurt, consider options, and begin a plan that will lead to healing. If you recognized a scene from your own life story when your child first told you about his or her hurt, and you are ready to share it, this might be a good moment. You might end your story by saying you believe the moment will come when your child will use this hurtful experience to offer someone else comfort, because that is the kind of caring person he or she is. And that is one of the many things you admire about him or her.

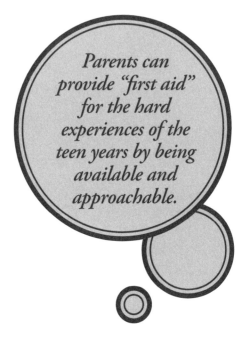

Parents can provide "first aid" for the hard experiences of the teen years by being available and approachable.

Seeing your child hurt is painful—that's a fact. But seeing the purpose in suffering makes it easier to bear. Someday your child will be an adult, probably a parent, and the training needed to handle that responsibility well occurs during the teen years. He or she is learning through experience and by example, and will be equipped to guide your grandchildren through the bumps and bruises of their lives, just as you are doing now.

Let's Talk

A line in a poem by Tennyson says, "Tis better to have loved and lost than never to have loved at all."

Why would somebody say that?

Can you remember a time in school when your feelings were hurt? What happened? How did you cope?

Is there someone in your class who always seems to be picked on or ignored? Have you wondered how that person feels, or how you might help the situation?

Do you know someone who cuts him or herself or is very thin and refuses to eat more? Has that person ever talked to you about his or her feelings?

Sometimes a boy will say that he will kill himself if the girl he likes refuses to go out with him anymore. What would you tell a girl in that situation to do? What would you do?

Have any of your friends ever told you that a boyfriend or even a girlfriend hit him or her? How did you respond? Would you tell somebody else? Why or why not?

If you were your own parent, and you learned that someone had mistreated you, how would you handle the situation? Why?

Let's Listen

Nehemiah 2   Psalm 13   Jonah   Hebrews 12

Let's Cook

COMFORT STUFFED PEPPERS

The most emotional conversations can be made a little easier if there's a diversion to work on together while you talk. Using your hands to mix the stuffing for a pepper can be messy, but it can also be a fun distraction. The chopping and mixing and preparation for something out of the ordinary like fondue or shish kabobs or a main dish salad will also offer lots of time together in the kitchen.

Comfort Stuffed Peppers

Serves: 4 | Prep Time: 15 Minutes | Cooking Time: 55 Minutes

Ingredients:

2	peppers (any color, but shape should be fit for stuffing)
1 lb.	ground beef
1	medium white onion, minced
8 oz.	canned tomato sauce (or 1½ C of your favorite spaghetti sauce)
2	eggs
½ C	white bread, torn into pieces
¼ C	fresh parsley, chopped
½ C	milk
¼ C	grated Parmesan cheese
1 Tbs.	salt
½ Tbs.	black pepper
1 tsp.	garlic powder
4 slices	provolone cheese (or ½ cup mozzarella cheese)

Instructions:

Preheat oven to 375 degrees. Set aside 4 tablespoons of tomato sauce for the end of the cooking process.

Prepare peppers by washing, cutting in half from stem to base, and cleaning away the seeds to create 4 cups. Set aside in baking pan. Prepare the stuffing by seasoning the ground beef with salt and pepper, minced onions, garlic powder, torn white bread, Parmesan cheese, milk, and remaining tomato/spaghetti sauce.

Using your hands to mix, combine all the ingredients thoroughly. Insert about ¼ pound of ground beef into each of the peppers. Place peppers back in baking pan, and cover with foil. Using a fork, poke a few holes in the foil to release steam. Place in oven. After 50 minutes, remove the peppers, and turn oven temperature to broil.

Using the tomato sauce you've set aside, spoon about 1-2 teaspoons over each pepper, and top off with cheese. Return peppers to broiler for another 3-5 minutes or until cheese melts and browns.

Serve over top of a bed of white rice.

A broken heart can use a different perspective. Why not enjoy a meal together someplace different—maybe on the porch or sitting on the floor in the den?

CHAPTER 17
Hopes and Hugs
MOVING OUT, MOVING ON

The LORD will guard you from all evil, will always guard your life.

The LORD will guard your coming and going both now and forever.

PSALMS 121:7-8

Of course you knew this moment would come. Parenting is intended to get sons and daughters ready to accept independence. The toddler you left in the church nursery; the first-grader you entrusted to a teacher; the scout you sent off to camp; the high school senior who made you proud. That young adult is now about to take on new responsibilities for his or her own life.

The day you take your child to that new residence is as significant in your family history as the day he or she was born. Moving out can be emotionally equivalent to cutting the umbilical cord. That first moment of physical autonomy was step one on the journey to this point.

You know that the bond between parent and child is never broken, and it is entirely possible that your child will return at some point to live under your roof; but it will never be the way it was. This moving out symbolizes moving on to adulthood, and the initial changes may be dramatic.

The rules by which your child will operate from now on are the rules he or she chooses to observe. Unless your child is attending a military academy, convent, seminary, or is on a team with a strict coach, no one at college has a personal interest in how well your child handles hygiene, cleanliness, or class assignments. No one will limit his or her consumption of soda or Snickers® or fries. No one will announce bedtime at a decent hour or make sure your child is awake in time for class. For a first-year student from a home where rules and responsibilities were the norm, the level of freedom can be shocking.

Take comfort in compassion, knowing the reality of these changes is as unsettling for your child as the thought of them is for you. Parents and children both shed tears during the breaking-in period schools call orientation. Well-run schools wisely require a first-semester class that covers time management and study skills, even interpersonal skills for managing roommate relationships, to smooth the adjustment process.

Wise parents welcome every phone call, listen intently, and practice their new role as consultant rather than manager by gently and positively reminding their child that he or she is living out a dream. Tell your child you know that he or she has everything necessary to succeed and you're confident about that because you pray daily. You might offer advice, but you must remind your child—and yourself—that the choices are his or hers, as are the consequences.

> *New levels of freedom can be shocking to first year students.*

Professionals in higher education are concerned about a trend in over-involved parenting. Too many parents are entangling themselves in their students' lives with countless calls and text messages. Their phone calls to administrators and professors and long-distance assistance with assignments and term papers rob their children of the opportunity to fully develop into the people they could become.

Perpetual adolescents never learn the important lessons of trying and failing. They never discover the range of gifts that God has given them, or test the possible options He may have for their lives beyond what is familiar to the family. They are reluctant to leave the comfortable nest, and their parents are content to let them stay. Parents who really want to get the full value of their investment in a child's college education will step back and let their child do the work of handling adult challenges. Allow your child the joy of doing well on his or her own. If you loosen your hold, your child can begin to manage life as an independent adult, and you can enjoy your new role as trusted advisor and confidant.

You need not fear that you will be forgotten or become irrelevant. As your child moves through life, all the lessons you taught and the love you gave will become more precious. You will hear yourself quoted, and if you watch closely you will see yourself modeled someday if your child is called to become a parent.

So let your child know that you will miss him or her, but also that you are excited to see what the future holds for both of you. Tell your child you are sure that no matter how geographically far apart your family may be, God will be with each of you, binding you together as you stay close to Him.

> *If you loosen your hold, your college student can begin to manage life as an independent adult, and you can enjoy your new role as a trusted advisor and confidant.*

Let's Talk

What do you expect to miss most about living at home with your parents when you move out on your own?
What are you looking forward to? How are you planning to stay connected to your family?

If you plan to attend college, what kind of school do you think you'd like best?
Have you talked to students or professors who teach subjects you might like to study?

Have you discussed plans to finance your higher education and learned about the
kinds of aid for which you might be eligible?

What would you want your roommate to be like?
What would be impossible for you to tolerate?

Some students "crash and burn" in college by making bad decisions.
What strategies can you rely on to help you reach your goals?

Many schools offer international study options. Is there a place you would like to explore?
What do you want to learn there?

Let's Listen

Genesis 37: 41-44   Jonah 1-4   Luke 3   2 Timothy 4

Let's Cook

HEARTY BEEF STEAK STEW

There will be plenty of time for that fall-back student diet of cheese crackers, ramen noodles, and cold pizza. Make this meal all about home-cooked favorites that are good enough to brag about. While you're getting the ingredients together, think of some other simple and nutritious meals that will keep a hard-working student in shape for those late-night study sessions.

Hearty Beef Steak Stew

Serves: 2 | Prep Time: 20 Minutes | Cooking Time: 25 Minutes

Ingredients:

6-8 oz.	steak (either New York strip or rib eye), cut in ½ inch cubes
1 clove	garlic, minced
½ tsp.	salt
¼ tsp.	pepper
2 Tbs.	vegetable oil
2 Tbs.	butter
3 Tbs.	all-purpose flour
5-7 C	beef or vegetable stock (or 5-7 cups of hot water with 2 beef bouillon cubes)
2 stalks	celery, cut ½ inch thick
3	carrots, cut into ½ inch sections
4	medium sized red potatoes, cut into ¼ inch cubes
2	green peppers, cut into ¼ inch pieces
1	medium onion, cut into 4 equal sections
1 pack	dried ramen noodles (optional, do not use the flavor pouch)

Instructions:

Add meat, salt, pepper, and flour to a large plastic bag. Seal and shake together.

In a pot or large saucepan, heat oil on high heat. Add garlic until lightly brown. Shaking off the flour from the meat, add the meat to the hot oil and sear 1-2 minutes on each side. Once the meat is seared, remove and set aside.

In the same pan, add the butter to the oil. When melted, create a roux by adding the rest of the dredging flour to the butter and oil, stirring together to create a paste. Add stock, one cup at a time, constantly stirring or whisking to create a smooth texture. Once incorporated, add the rest of the liquid, and turn the heat to medium. Add the meat and the rest of the vegetables. Let simmer uncovered until the potatoes are fork tender (approximately 20 minutes). Salt and pepper to taste.

For variations, continue reading on the next page...

Hearty Beef Steak Stew (continued)

Variations:

For a thicker stew, add less of the liquid (stock or water). For a soupier mix, add more water or stock, and also salt and pepper.

To make a beef and noodle dish, add the noodles from one pack of Ramen soup mix to the stew (do not use the flavor pouch). The noodles require only 2-4 minutes to cook fully. Serve with some crusty bread for a satisfying meal!

One-pot meals are easy to cook, easy to clean, and sure to please roommates and friends.

CHAPTER 18
Priceless

You formed my inmost being; you knit me in my mother's womb. I praise you, so wonderfully you made me; wonderful are your works! ...When I was being made in secret, fashioned as in the depths of the earth. Your eyes foresaw my actions; in your book all are written down; my days were shaped, before one came to be.

PSALM 139:13-16

Have you seen the *National Geographic* documentary that traces the growth of a human baby inside its mother's womb from the moment of conception to that moment when it is time to see Mom's face? It's a remarkable example of science catching up with Scripture to affirm what David knew by faith and celebrated over and over again in his psalms. We are not accidents. We're not even products of an impartial assembly line. We're handmade by God Himself. And, if that weren't enough, each of us is "fearfully and wonderfully" made, intricately woven according to God's plan for us. In his letter to the church in Ephesus, the Apostle Paul added that there was nothing last-minute about that plan; we were chosen for life before the foundation of the world. Paul goes on to remind us that the absolute proof of our worth is found in the work of Christ on our behalf. We really are priceless.

Knowing what we know, we can confidently draw some important conclusions about people of every age and condition. We're not disposable, and we're not burdens. We're here on purpose and for a purpose. We are meant to value life as much as we are valued.

Every child is a blessing from God. Every parent is entrusted with the responsibility to model God's love by protecting his or her baby's life from the moment its presence is known. This is not always easy. In fact, it can seem impossible, even under the best circumstances. But God has amazing resources for parents so they can discover the blessing He intends for them as they care for the children He places in their lives.

Because of God's perfect plan, no child can truly be called "unwanted" and no pregnancy "unexpected." Could the Giver of the Law create a child who could be labeled illegitimate?

> *We are not accidents. Each of us is fearfully and wonderfully made, intricately woven according to God's plan for us.*

Of course not! Is a child made in the image of God, our Creator and heavenly Father, ever really fatherless? No! We are not meant to be orphans, but heirs with Christ. We do not have to beg for scraps; there's a place with our name card already set at His table.

How might this knowledge shape our actions?

- It can give us confidence in God's wisdom when He instructs all of us to keep sexual relations inside marriage so we can be free to enjoy His blessings, including children, without the burdens that result from settling for less than His best for us.
- It can make us pro-life in a very practical way: We can decide that for our families, abortion is not a solution to a pregnancy.
- It can shape us as neighbors who welcome other children and their parents to our activities so they can see how God's love is expressed through families.
- It can turn us into activists who support the work of homes that offer counsel and shelter to young women who have chosen to either self-parent or release their child to adoptive parents.

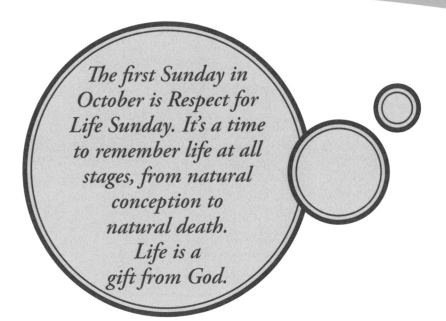

The first Sunday in October is Respect for Life Sunday. It's a time to remember life at all stages, from natural conception to natural death. Life is a gift from God.

It is truly amazing that the very basic gift we all have is life! Unfortunately the label "pro-life" has become politicized, and those who call themselves pro-life are often accused of being anti-choice. Honesty before the One who gives us life raises an important question: Do we truly recognize that our life is a gift from God? If the answer is "yes," there is no other choice than to be pro-life!

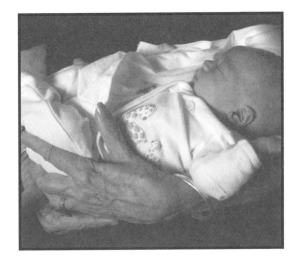

Let's Talk

Have you ever thought of yourself as priceless? How might that change your opinion of yourself?
Do you wonder what God might have been thinking when He picked out your hair or decided on your height?

Are other people really priceless?
If that's true, how might that affect the way we talk about them or treat them?

How do you think your parents would respond if you announced that you were pregnant or
had gotten someone pregnant? How would you want them to respond?

Have you ever thought of God's instruction that sex
be reserved for marriage as one of the ways He protects you?

What do you think is the hardest part about parenting when Mom or Dad are away from home?
How could you help somebody in that situation?

Let's Listen

Psalm 139   Ephesians 1   Job 38-42   Romans 8: 18-39

Let's Cook

HEARTY FOUR LAYER LASAGNA

For families with new babies, life is a blur of diapers and sleepless nights. Your unexpected gift of a real home-cooked meal would mean more than they can tell you. Make sure you've packed everything in containers that don't need to be rinsed and returned, or offer to come back later and do the dishes!

Hearty Four Layer Lasagna

Serves: 6 | Prep Time: 40 Minutes | Cooking Time: 90 Minutes

LAYER 1

Ingredients:

1 lb.	ground beef
½ tsp.	salt
¼ tsp.	pepper
1	medium onion, minced
1 Tbs.	olive oil
½ tsp.	garlic powder
2 C	spaghetti sauce

Instructions:

Heat pan with olive oil, and sauté onions. Add ground beef, and cook uncovered for about 10 minutes over medium-high heat, stirring until brown. Add the rest of the ingredients, and let cook for about 5 minutes. Set aside until ready to assemble.

LAYER 2

1	zucchini, chopped into ¼ inch cubes
1 tsp.	salt
½ tsp.	pepper
1 C	sour cream
1 C	ricotta cheese
½ Tbs.	butter
¼ C	breadcrumbs

In a separate pan, melt butter, add zucchini, and sauté until it becomes flexible. Do not cook fully through. Remove from heat, and place in a bowl. In the same pan, add sour cream, ricotta cheese, breadcrumbs, salt, and pepper. Mix thoroughly. Set aside until ready to assemble.

LAYER 3

1 box	frozen spinach, thawed and drained of excess water
1 Tbs.	olive oil
2 cloves	garlic, minced
½ tsp.	salt
¼ tsp.	pepper
¼ tsp.	red pepper chili flakes

In a separate pan, heat oil, and sauté garlic, adding salt, pepper, and red pepper chili flakes. Add the thawed and drained spinach, and sauté all together. Set aside until ready to assemble.

[Recipe continues on next page]

Hearty Four Layer Lasagna (continued)

LAYER 4

Ingredients:

¼ C	grated Parmesan cheese
¼ C	bleu cheese
¼ C	shredded provolone cheese
¼ C	heavy whipping cream
1 C	shredded mozzarella cheese
2 C	spaghetti sauce

Instructions:

Set aside the shredded mozzarella cheese for end of cooking process. Combine Parmesan cheese, bleu cheese, provolone, whipping cream, and spaghetti sauce. Set aside until ready to assemble. The mozzarella cheese will be the last topping of the lasagna.

ASSEMBLY INSTRUCTIONS

Use your choice of lasagna noodle (approximately 3-5 noodles per layer) and prepare according to instructions. Some lasagna noodles are ready to use, no boiling needed.

Lightly butter the bottom and sides of a 12-inch baking dish. When assembling the lasagna, pack in all of the various layers so the noodles and filling touch the sides of the pan. This will help keep the structure of each piece when cut.

Add one layer of lasagna noodles. Top and spread with the meat sauce. Add another layer of lasagna, and top off with an even spread of the ricotta–zucchini mixture. Add another layer of lasagna, and add the spinach mix. Add the final layer of lasagna noodle, and top off with the cheese combination, reserving the mozzarella for end of cooking process. This could be refrigerated until ready to bake.

When ready to cook, cover lasagna with foil, and bake in a preheated 375 degree oven for approximately 1 hour to 1 hour 15 minutes. Remove the lasagna from the oven. Remove the foil, and add the mozzarella cheese. Return to oven for another 10-15 minutes or until cheese is melted and bubbling. Wait 10-15 minutes before cutting and serving.

CHAPTER 19
Seeking Good

SUGGESTED FOR ALL HALLOWS' EVE — OCTOBER 31

In the morning sow your seed, and at evening let not your hand be idle:

For you know not which of the two will be successful,

or whether both alike will turn out well.

ECCLESIASTES 11:6

Just when you thought it was time for families like yours to give up on Halloween, with its increasing emphasis on horror movies and mischief, God puts a verse like this where it can't be missed. The assignment from the wise author of Ecclesiastes is to do good in the evening, too, and if ever there was an evening that needs the positive influence of God's people, it's Halloween!

In the eighth century, Pope Gregory IV declared that All Saints' Day would be observed on November 1. The night before this holy or "hallowed" day was designated All Hallows' Eve, a time to prepare for the commemoration of God's work in transforming ordinary people into extraordinary examples of faith.

Halloween can still be used for that good purpose if we remember that it was originally a holy day, not a scary one!

A teen-organized party for a local church, a neighborhood, or your extended family could introduce young children to real super heroes, such as the saints or servant-styled world leaders. With a parent offering behind-the-scenes assistance if it's needed, teens can provide an evening of games and fun that will be as enjoyable for the hosts as the kids they invite.

The satisfaction of creating the kind of event that will leave their young guests with happy memories will give teens a sense of their place and value in the bigger community.

Nobody understands the tug-of-war over Halloween better than our children, especially our teens. They're the target audience for dark films and video games that devalue life. Whereas Halloween was once a day when neighborhood kids could walk freely, it has become a day when "black magic" and the dark cults seem to have their greatest audience. Although we can't avoid

> *All Hallows' Eve was created as a time to prepare for the commemoration of God's work in transforming ordinary people into extraordinary examples of faith.*

children's desire to go trick-or-treating, we can encourage older children to see a deeper meaning in the day and the season.

A party (planned for the early part of the day when children trick-or-treat or on the weekend closest to Halloween) can provide teens with a chance to have fun, be with friends, and experience a deeper meaning of this celebration. Here's the twist: Teens plan the party not for themselves, but for younger siblings who are still too young to be exposed to the ugly scenarios that make Halloween less-than-hallowed.

Give teens an opportunity to be servants. Offer them a chance to exercise some responsibility rather than pull pranks. They're perfect for the job! Teens are young enough to know what younger kids will enjoy and what will bore them. Plus, they have the creativity to come up with the entertainment and the energy to keep up with the youngest guests. Teens will enjoy showing novices how to bob for apples or whistle with a mouthful of crackers. The messy process of making popcorn balls or caramel apples won't bother them. And when coaching relay teams or leading a scavenger hunt, they'll have as much fun as their guests.

If your teens ask for ideas, suggest that they have their elementary-age guests come dressed as a Bible character or a hero from church history. Younger guests will enjoy dressing up as part of God's creation—animal, vegetable, or even mineral! Suggest that they offer prizes for the most original costume or the best story about the character selected. Be sure to take lots of pictures and make them available to the grateful parents.

Enjoy the party and the satisfaction of giving the holiday back to the kids by overcoming evil with good. Praise your proactive teens for becoming heroes themselves! Imagine what a great compliment it would be if a younger brother or sister decided to dress up not like a goblin or a clown, but like his or her new hero—an older brother or sister!

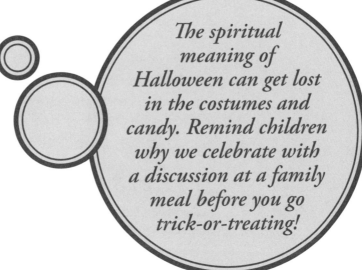

The spiritual meaning of Halloween can get lost in the costumes and candy. Remind children why we celebrate with a discussion at a family meal before you go trick-or-treating!

Let's Talk

Why do you think there's a market for horror movies? How did they get so connected to Halloween?

Some people keep their children from participating in Halloween activities because they are concerned for the children's safety. What are the pluses and minuses of that decision?

Who would you pick if you were going to dress up as a figure from the Bible or church history? What part of their story is most interesting to you?

Have you ever asked your parents about the ways their families celebrated Halloween when they were younger? What are their most vivid memories?

Do you know teens who are heavily involved in violent computer games? How does this hobby affect them? Why do the games seem so addictive?

When you become a parent, what rules will you have about watching movies or playing computer games? How will you handle the reality that your rules might be different from those of your child's friends?

Let's Listen

Wisdom 3:1-9   Ezekiel 37:1-14   Luke 24:36-43   Revelations 21:1-8

Let's Cook

PUMPKIN AND RICOTTA "WONTON-OLI"

When selecting foods for your kid-friendly party, incorporate healthy choices like fresh fall fruit along with the candy. Make sure the hosts will have enough energy to keep up with their guests

> *Pumpkin mix can also be used for savory foods, not just for sweet pies.*

by preparing a pre-party meal for them that takes advantage of the fall's best foods.

Pumpkin and Ricotta "Wonton-olis"

Serves: 4 | Prep Time: 30 Minutes | Cooking Time: 20 Minutes

Wonton-olis Ingredients:

40	wonton wrappers
1 C	ricotta cheese, strained
1 C	canned pumpkin pie mix
1	egg
1/4 tsp.	nutmeg
1 tsp.	salt
1/2 tsp.	pepper

Instructions:

Prepare the ravioli filling by combining ricotta cheese, eggs, nutmeg, pumpkin pie mix, salt, and pepper. Mix until all the ingredients are well incorporated.

Assemble the ravioli by separating the wonton wrappers on a tray lined with parchment or wax paper. Place 3/4 teaspoon of the mixture in the center of each wonton wrapper. Dip your finger in warm water and moisten the exposed wonton around the pumpkin filling. Flip one end of the wonton wrapper over to enclose the pumpkin mixture, gently pressing on the sides to seal it. Be careful to avoid air bubbles. The end result should look like small triangles with the pumpkin stuffing. Repeat this process until there are about 10 wonton-olis per person.

Place wonton-olis uncovered in refrigerator and let dry (or freeze for later use).

[recipe continues on next page]

Pumpkin and Ricotta "Wonton-olis" (continued)

Sage Butter Sauce Ingredients:

8	fresh sage leaves
4 Tbs.	salted butter
½ tsp.	salt
¼ tsp.	pepper
½ C	fresh Parmesan cheese, grated
½-1 C	warm starchy water (from the boiling ravioli)

Instructions (continued):

When ready to cook, boil a large pot of salted water and add the pumpkin stuffed wontons. Be sure not to overcrowd the pot. This generally means cooking 12-15 wontons at a time, depending on size of the pot. Let cook for approximately 5-7 minutes or until you see the wonton-olis start to float in the boiling water. Scoop them out and immediately sauté in the butter sage sauce. Reserve at least 1/2 cup of the starchy water for the sauce.

Prepare the sage butter sauce by melting the butter in a large frying pan. Add the fresh sage leaves and 1/2 teaspoon of salt. Add 1/2 cup of starchy pasta water to help thicken the sauce. Add the wonton-olis and let sauté in butter for 2-4 minutes. Add cheese and let melt. The sauce should thicken slightly but still remain somewhat soupy. Serve with crusty bread to help "mop up" the sauce!

To Serve Deep Fried

Heat 1/4 quart of vegetable oil over medium heat in a deep frying pan. Carefully add wonton-olis to the hot oil, making sure not to overcrowd the pan. Cook approx. 3-5 minutes per side. When both sides are brown, remove and place on paper towels to absorb excess grease. Sprinkle with salt immediately. Serve with your favorite dipping sauce (cheese, tomato, or sweet and sour work well).

CHAPTER 20

New Creations

For by grace you have been saved through faith, and this is not from you; it is the gift of God; it is not from works, so no one may boast. For we are his handiwork, created in Christ Jesus for the good works that God has prepared in advance, that we should live in them.

EPHESIANS 2: 8-10

"Amazing Grace, how sweet the sound that saved a wretch like me." Millions have sung those familiar words since John Newton wrote them in the 1700s. According to his own writings and the accounts of the day, Newton wasn't taking poetic license when he used the word "wretch" to describe himself. Before he was transformed by grace, he was famously profane, self-absorbed, cynical about spiritual things, and in pursuit of what is often called "riotous living." Newton had disappointed his father, abused his friends, and wasted his talents. If his mother had still been alive when Newton was a young adult, she would have wept. She was a believer, and her last moments with her seven-year-old son were spent in prayer for him to live a life of faith. But as he grew into his teens, he went in the exact opposite direction. John Newton was indeed a wretch, not unlike any of us who once walked our own paths away from the Savior.

The truth about God's love for us is that He knows our sinful nature apart from His transforming grace. He saw our helplessness and hopelessness and provided for our needs even when we were unable to ask. The Apostle John sums it up this way: "For God so loved the world that He gave His only Son, so that everyone who believes in Him might not perish but might have eternal life." By His life and sacrifice and resurrection, Jesus gives us life. It is a gift of grace, which is defined as unmerited favor.

When we believe, God gives us new life. We are no longer captive to sin. We are now counted among the saints.

That idea might amuse you at first because we use the word "saint" to refer to people who are exemplary models for the rest of us. Those people have been honored by the Church and presented as ideal heroes of the faith.

We have a hard time picturing ourselves in the same grouping, but in fact, when we are transformed by grace, we too become saints in the making. We become people who are willing to follow Christ and willing to live in obedience to His commands. We are changed, like John Newton and Saints Francis, Paul and Augustine were changed, from being eager to follow their own whims, to being eager to do what pleases our Savior. To evoke the Biblical image, when we are grafted onto the tree of life, we want to bear good fruit and plenty of it. As we mature in faith, we move from assuming we could never live like a favorite saint, to examining that saint's life and resolving to change so that we might better reflect Christ.

We live in a special time: the Church is considering the elevation of Blessed Mother

> *God doesn't call us to be successful; He calls us to be faithful.*

Teresa of Calcutta to Saint Teresa of Calcutta. She was our contemporary. Our knowledge of her life helps us to understand her humanity. She was a real person who needed a Savior just as we do. She did not set out as a believer to make herself a "headliner." On the contrary, she didn't have anything in mind but to follow where Christ led, even when that turned out to be the gutters of Calcutta. Her interest was in the good of others and the spread of the Gospel.

She kept her focus on Christ and obedience to His Word. Even the world's highest honors, including the Nobel Peace Prize, did not change her passion for society's cast-offs.

Pope John Paul II said of Mother Teresa, "She had chosen to be not just the least but to be the servant of the least." She used her fame as a tool to do still more for these people she was called to serve. She was compelled to show her faith through her works.

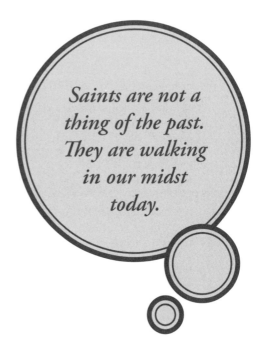

Saints are not a thing of the past. They are walking in our midst today.

We can be like that. John Paul II also said, "True holiness does not mean a flight from the world; rather, it lies in the effort to incarnate the Gospel in everyday life, in the family, at school and at work, and in social and political involvement." That's the outward expression of inward change. That's the secret of sainthood.

Let's Talk

What's your mental picture of a "saint?" Do you know what influences helped to form that picture? Would you call them positive or negative?

If you were to write a help-wanted ad for a saint, what qualities would you look for?

Among the people you know personally, who might you describe as having those qualities? Do you know if there was a time in their lives when those qualities weren't as obvious?

The Bible provides detailed information about the sins of people God calls His own, like King David and the Apostle Paul. Why would that information be important for us?

Is there someone in your circle of friends or family that people have declared hopeless? What might prompt you to keep praying when there's no reason to think the person is interested in change?

Many stories of transformation include incidents of success and failure. What lessons about God's power and purpose do you think we can learn from these stories and from our own successes and failures?

Let's Listen

Jonah 2   John 1   Romans 1:1-20

2 Corinthians 5   Galatians 6

Let's Cook

LAND, AIR, AND SEA PAELLA COMBINATION

Preparing delicious foods is all about transformation. Raw ingredients that often seem incompatible are prepared according to the recipe and go from inedible to delicious! A good meal is a gentle show-and-tell reminder that it is entirely possible to be transformed and that God will apply heat if needed to make the process complete.

> *Remember: Different meats in the same dish often require different temperatures and different cooking times.*

Paella

Serves: 8 | Prep Time: 20 Minutes | Cooking Time: 30 Minutes

Ingredients:

2 C	long grain rice
2	boneless chicken breasts, cut into ½ inch pieces
2	Spanish chorizo sausages (or Italian sausages), cut into ¼ inch cubes
12-15	pre-cooked frozen shrimp, thawed
1 Tbs.	dried cilantro
½ tsp.	saffron
1 tsp.	paprika
1 tsp.	Old Bay® Seasoning (or any dried seafood seasoning)
1 tsp.	salt and pepper
¼ C	extra virgin olive oil
4 cloves	garlic, finely minced
1	yellow onion, diced
1 C	canned diced tomatoes
2	bay leaves
2-4 C	water (depending on how quickly rice cooks)
2 C	Corona® or light beer (you can drink the rest)
1	eight-ounce can chopped clams in juice
3-4 Tbs.	fresh flat-leaf parsley leaves
2	lemons, sliced into 6-8 slices for garnish

[recipe continues on next page]

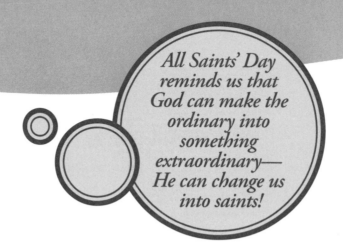

Paella (continued)

Instructions:

Mix the dry spice ingredients in a bowl, combining cilantro, paprika, saffron, Old Bay,® salt, and pepper. Season the chicken and sausage together with the dried spices and set aside.

In a separate bowl, mix the wet ingredients, combining the diced tomatoes, water, beer, and the can of chopped clams. Set aside.

Heat 4 tablespoons of olive oil in a large pan (or paella pan) over medium-high heat. Add the chicken and sausage and cook for 7-10 minutes or until brown. Remove meat and set aside (these will be fully cooked by the end of the cooking process).

Add the rest of the olive oil to the pan and heat. Add rice and cook for about 30 seconds to 1 minute or until the rice begins to take on some color. Add the garlic, onion, and bay leaves and sauté with rice until onions become translucent (approximately 1-2 minutes). Add the liquids to the pan and stir to mix all of the flavors together. Return the chicken and sausage to the pan and continue to cook for 15-20 minutes. Stir rice occasionally so that liquids simmer and the rice releases its starch. If liquids dry out too quickly before rice is soft, add 1 cup of hot water at a time and stir together.

Add shrimp and allow cooking to warm pre-cooked shrimp for 1-2 minutes. Rice should be moist but not soupy. Rice at bottom of pan may begin to brown and caramelize, which is the desired texture. Before serving, add fresh parsley and stir together. Serve with lemon wedges as garnish.

CHAPTER 21

Courage and Convictions

Now as you excel in every respect, in faith, discourse, knowledge, all earnestness,

and in the love we have for you, may you excel in this gracious act also…

For you know the gracious act of our Lord Jesus Christ, that for your sake

He became poor although He was rich, so that by His poverty you might become rich.

2 CORINTHIANS 8: 7-8

Imagine for a moment that you are Pietro Bernardone. You are a successful merchant and a leader in Assisi, your town in the beautiful region of Umbria, Italy. Your son Giovanni, who was nicknamed "Francesco" by his French mother, shows no interest in the family business, but until recently he has enjoyed the privileged lifestyle it provided. Lately, Francesco says he's had unusual dreams and even messages from God. After one of these messages, he took product out of your business inventory and sold it without your permission, along with the top-of-the-line transportation you had given him, and handed all the cash over to the local parish priest to fix up the church. The priest knew the money came from your resources, not your son's, and refused it. Your son responded by throwing the money on the ground.

When he learned you were angry, your son hid out for a month before you found him and brought him home. You grounded him, hoping he would come to his senses, but your wife let him out of the house, and he took refuge in a different church. Finally, to teach Francesco a lesson, you took him to court to cut off his inheritance, but Francesco declared that the court had no jurisdiction over him because God the Father is his true father. Francesco demonstrated the sincerity of his decision by removing all the clothing you provided for him and publicly renouncing all the human rights and comforts that would have been his. Francesco then went out into the hills beyond your hometown with no apparent plans for his future. The break has been total. You are at home without your son, wondering what would possess anyone, especially your own child, to walk away from the good life and welcome the prospect of poverty. You are sure he has traded his birthright for nothing of value.

From Pietro's point of view, his son was a failure. But with the benefit of historical perspective, we know better. Francesco was one of God's great successes. The story of his life has been told and retold from the thirteenth century to the twenty-first. Francesco's willingness to joyfully give up everything, do anything, and associate with anybody in order to show the love of Christ through his simple and pious life

> *Saint Francis' story offers proof that God provides for every need when we trust Him.*

remains a model of godly living. Francesco's only goal was to use his life of poverty to help others find real riches in their faith. He rid himself of everything that hindered his ability to focus on the work of God. He wanted nothing for himself, but God gave him fame and honor beyond anything he could have achieved as the most renowned merchant. Francesco died in October 1226, and by July 1228 Pope Gregory IX had canonized him in recognition of all the good he had done for the least in God's kingdom. Francesco, the son Pietro could not get to conform, is the blessed Santo Francesco, Saint Francis of Assisi.

The man who wanted nothing for himself is now honored everywhere. His simple life sermon urging penance, brotherly love, and peace has challenged millions of believers and fueled the vocations of generations of priests and nuns who have been called into the Orders he founded. They follow the humble example of Saint Francis by offering vows of poverty, chastity, and obedience to God. The good works of the Franciscans and the nuns of the Poor Clares, an order founded by St. Clare and inspired by Saint Francis, have been used by God on every continent.

Saint Francis' story offers so many lessons for families with teens. We see that God provides for every need when we trust Him. We have visible proof that the way to real happiness and contentment is not through the acquisition of things. And we're confronted with the fact that our children's future is not meant to be in our hands; their success might look like failure at first; the world might call them poor and inconsequential.

Saint Francis lived from 1182 until 1226. He is the patron saint of animals and is world famous, even to this day, for bringing hope to the weary.

By looking at the tug-of-war both Pietro Bernardone and Saint Clare's father, Favorino Scifi, Count of Sasso-Rosso, undertook in their attempts to keep their children from decisions they could not understand, we can see the futility of opposing God's plan. Loosen your grip, so God can hold your children close to Him.

Let's Talk

The first time Saint Francis was moved to help someone in need, the money he gave was his father's.

Why did this make his father so angry?

The first time Saint Francis had a dream, he saw sets of armor bearing crosses, and a voice said, "These are for your men." Saint Francis interpreted the dream to mean he would become a prince. Did he?

Church leaders opposed Saint Francis and Saint Clare when they insisted that they and the members of their orders own nothing, not just as individuals, but also as organizations.

What are the pros and cons of this position?

Have you ever heard someone say a task is "beneath his dignity?" What does that mean? Can it be true?

If Saint Francis lived in your neighborhood, who would be on his list of people to care for? What would he do for them? What might you do to follow his example?

If your parents absolutely opposed a decision you believed was directed by God, what would you do? How would you work toward a positive relationship?

Let's Listen

Deuteronomy 28:1-12   Psalm 27   Mark 12:28-34   2 Corinthians 9

Let's Cook

What better way to honor the life of Saint Francis than to do good for someone else? Is there someone in your church who is confined to a wheelchair? Can you minister to that person by washing windows or scrubbing floors? Does he or she need firewood for the

> *The juice of citrus fruit like oranges, lemons, or limes can add a unique flavor to savory dishes like sausage or pork.*

months ahead or help with winterizing? On the day of your helpful visit, bring along a meal that is sure to have a lot of leftovers. That way, you can quietly leave some provisions behind and extend your ministry without causing embarrassment.

Orange and Rosemary Pork Skewers

Serves: 6 | Prep Time: 75 Minutes (includes marinade) | Cooking Time: 30 Minutes

Ingredients:

6	skewers (wooden or metal)
2 lb.	pork roast cut into 1 inch thick cubes (measure to have 4-6 cubes per skewer)
1 tsp.	salt
½ tsp.	pepper
1	orange, juiced
1 Tbs.	orange zest
2 Tbs.	fresh rosemary leaves, minced (or 1 tablespoon dried rosemary)
3 Tbs.	olive oil
1 bag	pre-washed mixed field greens

Instructions:

Preheat oven to 375 degrees. Cut the pork into 1 inch cubes and place in a bowl. Combine salt, pepper, olive oil, orange zest, orange juice, and rosemary in a bowl. Add pork and marinate for about 1 hour.

Prepare skewers by adding 4-6 pieces of pork to each. Place skewers on a flat baking pan covered with aluminum foil. Pour extra sauce over the pork. Place in oven for 25-30 minutes, turning every 10 minutes. Serve hot skewers over the mixed field greens. Pour some of the hot marinade over greens to wilt and flavor them.

Tagliatelle ai Funghi Porcini

Serves: 4 | Prep Time: 15 Minutes | Cooking Time: 20 Minutes

Ingredients:

1 box	Tagliatelle pasta (a flat wide noodle—fettuccine is a good substitute)
1 sm. bag	dried porcini mushrooms (or mixed dried mushrooms)
1 C	white wine
½ C	olive oil (2 teaspoons oil for boiling water)
3 tsp.	salt (2 teaspoons for boiling water)
½ tsp.	black pepper
1-2 C	button mushrooms, chopped
2 cloves	garlic, minced
½ C	heavy whipping cream
1	pinch red chili peppers flakes
1 C	hot starchy pasta water for the sauce
2 Tbs.	fresh parsley, chopped
½ C	fresh grated Parmesan cheese

Instructions:

Boil 2 quarts of water with 2 teaspoons of salt. Add pasta and 2 teaspoons of oil and stir. Re-hydrate the dried mushrooms by first rinsing in cold water. Add the dried mushrooms to the white wine and put in the microwave for 1 minute, heating the wine and softening the mushrooms. Once cooled, remove the mushrooms from the wine (saving the wine) and chop the mushrooms finely. Set them aside.

In a separate pan, add olive oil, garlic, and chili flakes and sauté over medium heat. Add the chopped mushrooms and the button mushrooms and sauté, being careful to avoid splashing the hot oil.

When pasta is al dente, reserve 1 cup of starchy water. Drain the rest of the water from the pasta. Return the pasta to the pot, add the hot olive oil and mushroom mixture. Turn heat to medium and continue to cook the pasta with mushroom oil. Add the mushroom flavored wine and the reserved 1 cup of hot starchy pasta water to the pasta and let cook for about 1-2 minutes more. Add salt and pepper.

Generally, this pasta does not have a lot of sauce but just enough flavored oil to cover each noodle. Add grated Parmesan cheese, heavy whipping cream, and fresh parsley. Let cook for another 1-2 minutes. Toss sauce and pasta together and serve with some extra grated Parmesan cheese.

CHAPTER 22
Goodness and Mercy
SUGGESTED FOR THANKSGIVING DAY

Give thanks to God, bless his name; good indeed is the LORD,

Whose love endures forever, whose faithfulness lasts through every age.

PSALM 100: 4B-5

If Thanksgiving Day had an adjective, it would probably be "comfortable." There's something about the mood of the day that makes it easy to enjoy in any setting, with any group. Traditions may abound, but there are no "musts" that cannot be changed a bit from one year to the next, or changed back again by popular demand, without generating a family crisis. It is a totally transportable celebration that has been observed onboard the space shuttle orbiting the earth and in military mess tents around the globe. It's for families, friends, even total strangers who are united for a few hours to share a meal and the blessings of a day that has a clear and simple mandate—say thank you.

There are many diversions on Thanksgiving, and they seem to increase each year. Football games and parades have worked their way into the day, but they're fun to watch and have become a valued part of many gatherings. Some families tire of watching the television and hold their own annual touch football classics in the backyard. These games take family bonding to a whole new level.

Another distraction at Thanksgiving comes via magazine editors and home décor experts intent on convincing hosts that color coordinated place settings and table arrangements deserve more attention than the people gathered around the table. They want us to think that our china is able to do more for us than hold the cranberries.

So far, in spite of the pressures, most of us are refusing to trade the familiar for the fancy. Labor-intensive details like artfully arranging herb leaves to form a design under the skin of the turkey

> *Thanksgiving is a holiday with a clear and simple mandate—say thank you.*

have just not caught on with most cooks!

We know what matters most about Thanksgiving is being with the people for whom we are thankful. We appreciate the food, but when it comes to making our celebration memorable, the food does not compare with the company.

Family gatherings are not seamless productions. Your niece's recipe for lime gelatin salad may not improve with age. Your uncle's fondness for practical jokes may be as annoying as ever. Your cousin's date may go out of his way to make sure everyone knows his political views. But the flaws of today have a way of becoming the stories you'll share tomorrow as you recount your family history.

Thanksgiving Day reminds us that it's within the context of family that we learn how to appreciate and get along with people who don't share our opinions. In family we see that the process of aging can be both beautiful and difficult. Through family, we learn about bearing one another's burdens and sharing one another's joys; we find the strength to help with challenges we might have avoided if they faced a friend or neighbor. We learn to celebrate the fact that God picked this particular batch of less-than-perfect individuals to be our family. And when we see many of them gathered in one spot, joining hands to share a word of blessing over a meal that symbolizes all that God gives in response to our prayer for daily bread, we know what matters most to us and how we would start our list of that for which we are most thankful. Is it any wonder that the word "Eucharist"—Christ's sacred meal—literally means "thanksgiving?"

Your local Catholic Charities, Saint Vincent DePaul organization, or church can help you find places to volunteer or donate food.

Let's Talk

What is your best Thanksgiving Day memory?

What makes it so special to you?

If you were in charge of compiling this year's list of things for which your family is thankful, what would make the top ten?

Prioritizing people and possessions in the right order is sometimes a struggle. Why do you think this is?

In his letter to the Philippians, the Apostle Paul acknowledged that the people of that church were having a difficult time; he then said, "Rejoice in the Lord always. Again I shall say it, rejoice!" How is it possible to be thankful or joyful when things do not seem to be going well?

Can you remember a circumstance that seemed awful when it happened but resulted in something good?

One of our national traditions is our attempt to ensure that everyone gets a Thanksgiving dinner. How would you feel if you were serving a meal at a homeless shelter and knew that some of your guests might be searching the dumpsters for their next meal?

Let's Listen

I Chronicles 16   Ezra 3   Psalm 100

2 Corinthians 9   Philippians 4

Let's Cook

SAGE MARINATED TURKEY BREAST
WITH CREAMY MINT CRANBERRY SAUCE
ROASTED POTATOES & FENNEL IN ANCHOVY BUTTER

Your Thanksgiving Day menu may be as much an heirloom as your family album. If you know your family won't be thankful for any change from their familiar green-bean casserole and bread stuffing, save these terrific recipes for another time when you want to celebrate the bounty God provides for our fellowship around the table.

Cooking parts of a turkey instead of a whole turkey at once is easier, saves time and reduces leftovers.

Sage Marinated Turkey Breast

Serves: 4 | Prep Time: 15 Minutes | Cooking Time: 40 Minutes

Ingredients:

4	large boneless turkey breast cutlets (approx. 1 inch thick)
1 C	seasoned breadcrumbs
1 tsp.	salt
½ tsp.	pepper
4 Tbs.	olive oil
1 Tbs.	butter
1 Tbs.	fresh sage leaves, finely chopped
1 Tbs.	flour
½ C	white wine
½ C	water

Instructions:

Preheat oven to 375 degrees. Season turkey breast on both sides with salt and pepper and cover with breadcrumbs. In a frying pan, heat olive oil over high heat. Add the breasts and sear for 2 minutes on each side. Remove and set aside.

In the same pan, turn heat to medium and add butter, chopped sage, and flour to create a roux. Slowly add white wine and water, whisking to break up lumps. Let simmer and thicken. Pour sauce over the turkey and cover with foil. Place in oven for approximately 35-40 minutes.

Creamy Mint Cranberry Sauce

Serves: 4 | Prep Time: 5 Minutes | Cooking Time: 15 Minutes

Ingredients:

2 Tbs.	butter
I Tbs.	sugar
I Tbs.	flour
8 oz.	canned cranberry dressing
¼ C	dried cranberries
2 C	heavy whipping cream
I tsp.	fresh mint, finely chopped
¼ tsp.	salt

Instructions:

Melt butter in a saucepan over medium heat. Add the mint leaves, sugar, salt, and flour to thicken the butter and create a loose paste. Slowly add the 2 cups of heavy whipping cream, whisking to prevent lumps. Add canned cranberry dressing, breaking it up to create a creamy pink sauce. Add dried cranberries and let come to a soft boil. Ladle 2-3 tablespoons over the turkey.

Roasted Potatoes and Fennel

Serves: 4 | Prep Time: 15 Minutes | Cooking Time: 30 Minutes

Ingredients:

4	medium-sized red potatoes, cut in halves (or ¼ inch cubes)
4	fennels, cleaned and cut into ½ inch sections
2 cloves	garlic, minced
4-5 Tbs.	salted butter
2	anchovy fillets, minced
I tsp.	salt
½ Tbs.	black pepper
2 tsp.	parsley, fresh chopped

Instructions:

Preheat oven to 375 degrees. In a saucepan, sauté minced anchovies, butter, and garlic over medium heat. In a baking dish, add potatoes and fennel. (The fennel will break up like an onion, so there is no need to be exact with the 1/2 inch pieces. Do not use the fennel stem and leaves for this recipe.)

Once the anchovy butter is melted, pour it over the potato and fennel mixture. Season with salt and pepper. Place in oven. After 20-25 minutes, turn the oven to broil for about 5 minutes or until edges begin to brown. Sprinkle parsley as garnish and fresh flavoring before serving.

CHAPTER 23

'Tis the Season

SUGGESTED FOR THE ADVENT SEASON

A voice cries out: In the desert prepare the way of the LORD! Make straight in the wasteland a highway for our God! Every valley shall be filled in, every mountain and hill shall be made low; the rugged land shall be made a plain, the rough country, a broad valley. Then the glory of the LORD shall be revealed, and all mankind shall see it together.

ISAIAH 40: 3-5

Did you know there's a vaccine that prevents the hard-to-define disappointment and emptiness so many people feel when the Christmas tree comes down? It's found in Advent.

Advent is a time of spiritual preparation and anticipation. It provides a solid framework families can use to protect Christmas from being drained of its true meaning and spiritual blessings. Observing Advent at home and at church creates family time in the weeks before Christmas. When you pause to celebrate Advent, you focus on God's promises about the coming of Christ and anticipate the family Christmas traditions that mean the most to you.

Looking at the Old Testament prophesies and the richness of their detail, we see how intimately God is involved in the planning of Christ's Incarnation. Our holiday preparation is truly holy-day preparation, which should be marked by a wise investment of our time and resources rather than a waste of them.

Celebrating Advent at church and at home in our devotions, or by using a traditional Advent wreath or calendar to mark each day until Christmas, helps strengthen our ability to resist the clutter. When we appreciate the beauty of the real story of Christmas, we are able to put everything else in perspective.

The world pulls hard on us, attempting to divert our attention, our energy, and our budget, enticing us to join the frenzy called the holiday season. It offers a distorted shell of the real holiday, emptied of the very reason for the existence of Christmas. On the outside, it's all glitter and excitement; at its core, it's empty and melancholy. Advent is our life raft on a sea of sale circulars, invitations, skating elves, and inflatable snowmen.

Advent provides a solid framework families can use to protect Christmas from being drained of its true meaning.

Advent shows us that giving and receiving gifts is not an end in itself, but a representation of God's unmatchable gift to us. Advent reveals the importance of the genealogy recorded in the first chapter of the New Testament. Advent introduces the participants in the original nativity pageant. Advent tells us why the Magi were on their search; why Herod was worried; why Jesus had to be born in Bethlehem; and why we must not go along with the crowd, secularizing an event that is quintessentially sacred.

Week by week, we can make our homes and events a refuge for those who want to experience the true spirit of the season. We can gently point the way to a celebration that will not leave a bad aftertaste. We can create an environment where holiday memories will be of time spent with friends and loved ones. We can orient our sons and daughters to find the enjoyment in giving, especially in giving of their time and abilities. The genuine appreciation on the face of a child receiving his first toy reminds us of how many gifts we have taken for granted. By making the most of Advent, we can ensure that the Christmas spirit will linger in our homes long into the new year. Ultimately, Advent is a time to prepare for the greatest gift imaginable. The gift is not a what, but a who!

Advent begins four Sundays before Christmas. It's a time of patience, waiting, and prayer! Prepare well for Christmas by not rushing Advent.

Let's Talk

What is your favorite family tradition between Thanksgiving and Christmas? What makes it special?

You've grown up being told it is "more blessed to give than to receive." How can that be true?

If your family decided to not spend money on gifts for each other and donate that money instead, what are some gift ideas that don't cost anything? Where would you want the donation to go?

Have you ever thought about Jesus' human ancestors? Why do you think their names are in the Bible? Does anybody in your extended family keep track of your family tree? Have you ever been surprised by something you've learned about your heritage?

If you could change one thing about the holiday season, what would it be?

How does knowing that specific prophesies were fulfilled in Christ's birth affect your interest in the prophesies of His return?

Let's Listen

Genesis 3:15   Genesis 22   Psalm 72   Isaiah 7

Micah 5:2   Matthew 1   Luke 1

Let's Cook

MEATBALLS IN CREAMY VODKA SAUCE

Give your family the gift of time together this season. Simple meals that take advantage of the Crock-Pot or the microwave reduce prep time so you can have more time around the table, catching up with one another. Save some money and take advantage of your family's love of good food by creating custom gifts of cookies, jams, baked goods, soup mixes, pasta dinner baskets, or collections of your favorite recipes. Gifts like these are fun to make and wonderful to receive.

Meatballs

Serves: 6 | Prep Time: 20 Minutes | Cooking Time: 20 Minutes

Ingredients:

2 lb.	ground beef
1	onion, finely chopped
½ tsp.	garlic powder
½ tsp.	salt and pepper
2	eggs
¼ C	Italian bread crumbs
2 Tbs.	soy sauce
1 C	all-purpose flour
4 Tbs.	olive oil

Instructions:

Use your hands to combine ground beef, onions, garlic powder, salt, pepper, eggs, breadcrumbs, and soy sauce in a bowl. When thoroughly mixed, shape into meatballs about the size of golf balls. Roll them in flour and shake off excess. Heat olive oil over medium heat in a skillet and add meatballs. Cook until brown on all sides. Set aside to cool.
(Note: *After cooling, you can freeze them for use in another recipe, such as meatball subs.*)

To Serve as Subs

Preheat oven to 375 degrees. Toast regular sub rolls in the oven for 3-5 minutes. Brush buns with olive oil and add 3-4 meatballs per bun. Top with fresh mozzarella cheese and heat in oven for another 2 minutes to melt the cheese.

To Serve as Appetizers

Place meatballs in a flat dish with a small bowl of vodka sauce [*recipe on the following page*] for dipping. Place toothpicks next to this tray, as well as some pita bread wedges or slices of French baguette.

Vodka Sauce

Serves: 6 | Prep Time: 20 Minutes | Cooking Time: 20 Minutes

Ingredients:

1 Tbs.	olive oil
2 cloves	garlic, minced
1	medium-sized white onion, minced
2 Tbs.	fresh parsley, chopped
32 oz.	tomato sauce
1	6-ounce can tomato paste
1 C	heavy whipping cream
½ C	vodka
½ tsp.	salt
¼ tsp.	black pepper
3 pinches	red pepper flakes

Instructions:

Heat olive oil in a large pot or pan over medium heat. Sauté garlic, onions, and parsley until onions become translucent, approximately 2-3 minutes. Add tomato sauce, tomato paste, and 1 cup of heavy whipping cream. Stir well. Add salt, pepper and finally the vodka. Continue to stir and let simmer for about 2-3 minutes or until the smell of alcohol is not as strong. Add meatballs—enough to be covered by the sauce. Continue to cook with lid slightly off in order to release some steam. Let simmer for at least 10 minutes, letting the sauce take in the flavors of the meatballs.

Ask your children to help in the kitchen by cooking or cleaning up after a party. It's a gift I'm sure all parents would enjoy!

CHAPTER 24
Joy, Joy, Joy
SUGGESTED FOR THE CHRISTMAS SEASON

For God so loved the world that he gave his only Son, so that everyone who believes in him might not perish but might have eternal life. For God did not send his Son into the world to condemn the world, but that the world might be saved through him.

JOHN 3: 16-17

Do your holiday decorations include a crèche? Can you picture that incredible moment? God loves us so much that He willingly sent Jesus, His only Son, to be one of us, to live among us, and die for us so that we could live with Him forever. It is a gift of such enormity that there are not words to describe it.

To help us grasp the wonder of this event that changed the course of human history, the Apostle John begins his Gospel in this way: "In the beginning was the Word, and the Word was with God, and the Word was God. He was in the beginning with God. All things came to be through Him, and without Him nothing came to be. What came to be through Him was life, and this life was the light of the human race… And the Word became flesh and made His dwelling among us, and we saw His glory, the glory as of the Father's only Son, full of grace and truth." The Light of the World was born into the humblest of circumstances in a place called Bethlehem. He made His dwelling with us.

Consider that as you celebrate Christ's birth. The Light of the human race, God the Son, made

Himself at home with us. That is the reason for Christmas. Nothing else we associate with the holiday comes close to this. It doesn't matter if there is a single present under the tree—or even if there is a tree at all. It doesn't matter if the house is packed full of kids, or if circumstances keep you from gathering together. Nothing about your personal situation, not the sadness of separation, not illness or death, not poverty, nothing can cast a shadow on the celebration of the birth of our Savior and King.

> *When Christ is the center of the celebration, everything else about this holy day and the season surrounding it falls into its proper place.*

When Christ is the center of the celebration, everything else about this holy day and the season surrounding it falls into its proper place. The giving and receiving of gifts becomes what it should be, symbolic of the ultimate Gift and not an end in itself. The popular stories about Santa Claus, the Grinch, Rudolph, elves, and all the fictional characters who have crept into the season are moved from center stage to their subsidiary place with the tinsel and twinkling lights. From there, parents can choose to ignore these stories or include them without letting fiction supplant truth. Parents are free to explain to their children from the very beginning that the Christmas presents they receive are given by people who love them, and that they represent God's unconditional love for all of His children.

This freedom to celebrate the heart of the holiday releases your family from the crazed competitions that measure winners and losers by the height of the tree, the wattage of the lawn display, the size of the stack of packages, and the balance due on the credit cards. All of that is replaced with the simple pleasures of family time and family traditions, new and old, which put the emphasis on giving instead of getting.

Give your kids the gift of simple pleasures like a cookie-making party with their friends (be sure to make lots of extras for guests to take home for their parents). Organize the neighbors for an evening of caroling, followed by hot cocoa at your place. Decorate a tree for the birds who visit your yard in winter. Ask your local Christmas bureau for the name of a family in need. Buy gifts for each of them (and fewer for each other). Open your home to someone who would otherwise spend Christmas alone. Sometime during the Christmas season, read the Christmas story together. End it with a quiet moment that brings you back to the manger to sing with the angels and bow with the Magi. O come let us adore Him!

Christ has come!
Merry Christmas!
Maligayan Pasko! Feliz
Navidad! Joyeux Noel!
Buone Feste Natalizie!
Kala Christouyenna!
Sung Tan Chuk Ha!
Joy to the World!

Let's Talk

When you were younger, what part in the nativity pageant did you most want to have? What was its appeal? Have you ever wondered what it would have been like to be at the actual nativity?

What is your favorite Christmas memory? Does Christmas sometimes seem less fun as you get older? Have you thought about why or how it could be more fun again?

Some people go into a lot of debt to buy Christmas presents. Why would they do that? What are some alternatives?

How do you feel when you and your friends compare Christmas presents? Do you think that conversations like that are harder for some of your friends than others?

What's the oddest Christmas present you ever got? What's the most unique gift you ever gave? Why is giving and receiving gifts part of Christmas, not some other holiday?

Christmas makes some people depressed. How can you or your family encourage people who are having a hard time coping while others are celebrating?

Let's Listen

Isaiah 9:1-7   Matthew 2   Luke 2

John 1   Hebrews 1

Let's Cook

SAUSAGE AND SAGE STUFFED CORNISH GAME HENS
CREAMY BAKED BREAD AND ROOT VEGETABLE SIDE STUFFING

Have you ever considered the many moments we know about in Jesus' life that are connected to meals? He blessed the loaves and fishes and fed the multitude; He hosted the Passover meal and established the sacrament of Holy Communion; after His resurrection, He greeted His disciples with breakfast when they returned from fishing in the Sea of Galilee. At that meal, our Savior said to the Apostle Peter, "Feed my sheep." Over and over He invites us to His table to receive the bread of life. This Christmas remember to praise the Father for the gift of Christ and make Him the honored guest at your table.

Sausage and Sage Stuffed Cornish Game Hens

Serves: 6 | Prep Time: 15 Minutes | Cooking Time: 80 Minutes

Filling for Poultry

Ingredients:

2	sausages (approx. 8 oz.), cooked according to instructions and cooled and finely chopped into small pieces
5	fresh sage leaves
2 C	bread crumbs
2 Tbs.	mayonnaise
1 tsp.	orange zest

Instructions:

Combine all of these ingredients together, making a paste-like stuffing. Set aside in order to prepare the game hens.

Preparing Cornish Game Hens

Ingredients:

6	game hens
3 Tbs.	olive oil
1	orange, cut into 6 wedges
2 tsp.	salt
1 tsp.	pepper
2 tsp.	paprika

Instructions:

Wash and clean game hens at room temperature. Discard innards or freeze for future recipes. Dry hens with a paper towel. Drizzle extra virgin olive oil to lightly coat the exterior of each hen. Salt and pepper both inside and outside each hen. Sprinkle paprika over hens and rub with hands to evenly distribute seasoning. Insert one orange wedge and one large spoon of the stuffing to fill cavity. Set aside and prepare side stuffing.

[recipe continues on next page]

Creamy Baked Bread And Root Vegetable Side Stuffing

Serves: 6 | Prep Time: 15 Minutes | Cooking Time: 90 Minutes

Ingredients:

8 slices	white bread, cut or "ripped" into ¼ inch squares
2 stalks	celery, cut into ¼ inch pieces
2	carrots, cut into ¼ inch pieces
1	apple, cut into ¼ inch pieces
¾ C	dried cranberries
1	green pepper, cut into ¼ inch pieces
1	onion, cut into ¼ inch pieces
1 C	heavy whipping cream (or milk)
1 C	white wine
1 C	chicken broth
1 tsp.	salt
1 tsp.	black pepper
2 Tbs.	melted butter

Instructions:

Spray bottom and sides of a large baking dish with nonstick spray. Incorporate all of the ingredients together and mix thoroughly. Place each hen on top of a bakers rack over top of the stuffing leaving 1-2 inches between each hen. The juices of the hens will continue to drip onto the stuffing.

Cover the whole dish with aluminum foil and place in a 400 degree oven. After 50 minutes, drop the oven temperature to 375 degrees. Remove the foil and continue to cook for another 30 minutes. Baste every 10-15 minutes.

To baste: Use a saucepan to melt 2 tablespoons of butter with 1 cup of chicken stock or broth. Let this come to a slight simmer and use a brush to baste the hens. Cook hens according to instructions per weight or until you see the juices run clean when pierced with a fork. The juices from the hens and the basting liquid will continue to drip onto the bread stuffing and cook all of the ingredients so the flavors run together. After hens are cooked, remove and let rest for about 10-15 minutes. Mix stuffing and let cook in oven for another 10-15 minutes.

~Journal~

Date ....

....

Participants ....

....

....

....

Dishes Enjoyed ....

....

....

....

Memorable Conversation ....

....

....

Notes For Next Time ....

....

....

Date..
....

Participants..
....
....
....

Dishes Enjoyed..
....
....
....

Memorable Conversation..
....
....
....

Notes For Next Time..
....
....
....

Date ....
....

Participants ....
....
....
....

Dishes Enjoyed ....
....
....
....

Memorable Conversation ....
....
....
....

Notes For Next Time ....
....
....
....

Date..

....

Participants..

....

....

....

Dishes Enjoyed..

....

....

....

Memorable Conversation..

....

....

....

Notes For Next Time..

....

....

....

Date ....

....

Participants ....

....

....

....

Dishes Enjoyed ....

....

....

....

Memorable Conversation ....

....

....

....

Notes For Next Time ....

....

....

....

Date ....

....

Participants ....

....

....

....

Dishes Enjoyed ....

....

....

....

Memorable Conversation ....

....

....

....

Notes For Next Time ....

....

....

....

Date..

....

Participants...

....

....

....

Dishes Enjoyed..

....

....

....

Memorable Conversation..

....

....

....

Notes For Next Time..

....

....

....

Date ....

....

Participants ....

....

....

....

Dishes Enjoyed ....

....

....

....

Memorable Conversation ....

....

....

....

Notes For Next Time ....

....

....

....

Date...
....

Participants...
....
....
....

Dishes Enjoyed...
....
....
....

Memorable Conversation...
....
....
....

Notes For Next Time..
....
....
....

Date ....
....

Participants ....
....
....
....

Dishes Enjoyed ....
....
....
....

Memorable Conversation ....
....
....
....

Notes For Next Time ....
....
....
....

Date . . . .

. . . .

Participants . . . .

. . . .

. . . .

. . . .

Dishes Enjoyed . . . .

. . . .

. . . .

. . . .

Memorable Conversation . . . .

. . . .

. . . .

. . . .

Notes For Next Time . . . .

. . . .

. . . .

. . . .

Date ....

....

Participants ....

....

....

....

Dishes Enjoyed ....

....

....

....

Memorable Conversation ....

....

....

....

Notes For Next Time ....

....

....

....

Recipe Index